ADVANCE ACCLAIM

There is a growing awareness about the importance of breathing and breath regulation through yoga (pranayama). Renu Mahtani, a physician trained in conventional medicine but with a deep commitment to yoga practice and therapy has succeeded in blending science, ancient wisdom from the yoga texts, and practical knowledge, in a way which is unusual and makes the book 'Power Pranayama' definitely worth reading. Technical terms are dealt with in a way which can be easily understood by a person with no specific knowledge of medicine. The book has many therapeutic applications of *pranayama*.

—Shirley Telles MBBS, Ph.D.,
Director of Research
Patanjali Yogpeeth, Haridwar, India

As a regular and long-standing practitioner of Pranayama for the last half a decade, I have experienced and enjoyed its benefits. But even for a practitioner like me, the book proved to be an extremely useful read.

The book brings out the theoretical and practical aspects of Pranayama. It is enriched by perceptive quotes from various authorities. It provides the logic for various parts of Pranayama and also indicates the potential benefits. Dr. Renu Mahtani brings her expertise both as a qualified MD and as a passionate teacher of Pranayama.

My compliments to Dr. Mahtani for such an excellent book. I would strongly recommend this book to anyone who has an interest in living a healthy life.

—Ravi Pandit
Chairman & Group CEO
KPIT Cummins Infosystems Ltd.

Indian sages of yore have given the science of Yoga and Pranayama to give the agitated human mind some tranquility and help elevate its Godliness. In this book, the whole science and the art of the procedures are explained in lucid language for the reader to follow in his own way. I recommend this book very strongly. It gets very high marks in my assessment. May Dr. Renu's book be the beacon light for practitioners of those sciences for all times to come.

—Padma Bhushan
Prof. B.M. Hegde, MD, FRCP, FRCPE,
FRCPG, FRCPI, FACC, FAMS.
Retd. Vice Chancellor, Manipal University
Editor-in-Chief, The Journal of the Science of
Healing Outcomes
Chairman, State Health Society's Expert Committee
Former Prof. Cardiology, The Middlesex Hospital
Medical School, University of London
Affiliate Prof. of Human Health, Northern Colorado University
www.bmhegde.com

The book is probably, the best ever Handbook of *Pranayama* for Health, Happiness and Harmony. It contains everything right from conscious breathing to the state of a total Self harmony, all attainable through the methodical process of *Pranayama*. The author communicates that the breath is the physical counterpart of *the mind* and the act of conscious breathing is verily *the mind* in a positive action. It holds a very practical promise to the modern man, showing how breath is the vehicle to identify stress, as well as, an unfailing barometer of relaxation. The implications of *Pranayama* to the brain and mind and to common disorders of health, have been dealt with most pragmatically.

—Dr. R.S. Bhogal,
Principal, G. S. College of Yoga & Cultural Synthesis,
Kaivalyadhama, Lonavla-410403

Power Pranayama

Discover the healing potential of your breath

INCLUDES FREE DVD

Dr. Renu Mahtani M.D.

FOREWORD BY KIRAN BEDI, Ph.D.

JAICO PUBLISHING HOUSE

Ahmedabad Bangalore Bhopal Chennai
Delhi Hyderabad Kolkata Lucknow Mumbai

Published by Jaico Publishing House
A-2 Jash Chambers, 7-A Sir Phirozshah Mehta Road
Fort, Mumbai - 400 001
jaicopub@jaicobooks.com
www.jaicobooks.com

POWER PRANAYAMA
With DVD
ISBN 978-81-8495-153-0

First Jaico Impression: 2010
Fourth Jaico Impression: 2011

Printed by
Rashmi Graphics
#3, Amrutwel CHS Ltd., C.S. #50/74
Ganesh Galli, Lalbaug, Mumbai-400 012
E-mail: tiwarijp@vsnl.net

I dedicate this book to
the universal healing force and
all the people who opened my eyes to it.

CONTENTS

FOREWORD

Breath could be called the 'wonder drug', a panacea to our modern time problems of health – physical, intellectual and emotional! Pranayama and breath awareness have stood the test of time and now even scientific researchers are proving their value and uniqueness.

Written by Dr. Renu Mahtani, MD (Medicine), a practicing physician from Pune, 'Power Pranayama – Discover the healing potential of your breath' is a knowledge based book, with a strong foundation of relevant anatomy, physiology and the body-mind dynamic. The techniques and the concepts are supported with logical explanations to satisfy the quest of our ever-enquiring mind.

The book deals with the transforming power of Pranayama in a very scientific way, not just for the body but also for the mind. The educated young and middle aged professionals are commonly facing mental unrest, irritability, emotional lability, insomnia, lack of energy and ill health! Devoting just 15 minutes a day to Pranayama can transform them and improve their performances in their respective fields with a positive drive!

The importance of good breathing, breath awareness and mind management, is the need of the time, not just to keep the body fit, but also to get a focused and balanced mind-set for success in any avenue of life!

— Dr. Kiran Bedi, *Indian Police Service*

ACKNOWLEDGEMENTS

I thank The Supreme for giving me situations in life that have helped broaden my mindset and approach towards health.

I am grateful to all my family and friends who loved me even more when I was hating myself for my skin disease. I am indebted to each and every person sent in this journey to help me heal and those who taught me various aspects of healing.

- Mr. Avinash Khare for sowing the seeds of Pranayama in me.

- Dr. Nagarathna didi from SVYASA, Bangalore for being my mentor! It is you who encouraged me to take my first step towards teaching Yoga and Pranayama.

- Nischala Joy Devi, my first international Yoga teacher, who taught me compassion in Yoga as the most important ingredient for connecting with patients.

- Ramdev baba for re-awakening the world towards the need for Pranayama

- Dr. David Shanahoff Khalsa from the University of California, San Diego for his extensive scientific research in Pranayama. The evidences have validated the authenticity of this ancient science. You are my 'Breath Therapy' Guru, Sir.

- My mother-in-law who even at the age of 83, keeps encouraging me! I can never forget how you helped me on the home front when I was studying medicine!

- My husband Raju for giving me everything with joy to turn my passion into reality. I value all your suggestions and criticisms to make me more stable on this path.

- My children Riya, Raunak and Munna for loving me unconditionally. Thanks for all your sacrifices to see that the classes go on smoothly.

- My mother Chitra and brother Rajesh for promptly sending from the US any book or course material I want, to keep me updated with the global trends and progress in this field.

- My soul-sister Sujata Nerurkar who came in to join hands when I needed a like-minded partner, keen to spread quality Yoga. You have really helped make the difference.

- Roseleen Sahni for being our young face of Yoga with all the power and passion to pull the youth towards this unbeatable science. Thanks for helping me for this book by posing so gracefully for the postures.

- Mehendi Mangwani, for your calm and steady poise in the video showing the special Pranayama and breathing practices with focussed therapeutic value.

- Dr. Tejaswini Gholap, for sparing her time from her dental practice to be our main model for the video shooting. Your elegance and grace is unmatched!

- Mr. Hari Bhargava, a very successful entrepreneur and my first Pranayama student, for allowing us to shoot the video in his beautifully landscaped property.

- Baasu Palkar with his team — Pramod and Sanjay for their talent through the lens and the video editing skills.

- Ashwina Vakil for her intelligent editing of the manuscript.

Without all the many clients who have come to me with full trust, I would not have become a better person and doctor. I have learnt something or the other from each one of you.

Thank you every one to make this project happen!

INTRODUCTION

To all who are about to read this book – may we find and
become aware of the truth in ourselves.

—*Eckhardt Tolle*

Healing is a Journey

What led me to discover the amazing healing power of pranayama

I am one of the blessed ones – a physician who is still evolving towards the better. Practicing medicine is not just a profession for me but a platform that has brought me closer to humanity.

With time, my approach towards health has changed. The vision towards illness and health is getting wider day-by-day. I have realised that illnesses don't come to us, but that we are the ones who create an inviting environment for them. Everything contributes to our health – how we work, our activities, what and how we eat, how we think, our emotions and relationships, and our attitude towards life.

In the normal course of life we take our health for granted; it is only when we are struck by a chronic disease that we wake up. Resorting to medical help is the first step for most of us as symptom relief is of prime concern. However, medicines can keep the situation under control but cannot eradicate the disease. The symptoms resurface if the treatment is stopped and often, despite taking medication, things move from bad to worse. It is only then, and usually out of compulsion, that we decide to adopt a different lifestyle. The first step is to eat healthier food and engage in regular exercise, and we are pleased to observe that our attitude to good health has a new zeal, a new hope.

On seeing people whose health did not improve despite taking medicines, watching their diet, exercising and doing the things one normally does during an illness, I started to realise that we doctors are not really justifying our identity as healers. We prescribe medicines that can reduce the symptoms superficially or maybe modulate the disease. However we have no control over, and honestly do not know how to avoid, the side effects of medicines. How can we then talk of curing someone?

My own affliction – psoriasis, a chronic, nagging stubborn skin disease was an eye opener! I came to realise that looking at the site of disease, i.e., lungs for asthma, joints for arthritis, and skin for psoriasis, is very superficial. What we see and perceive is the physical evidence of something actually happening deeper inside. One can treat the ailment with medicines at the physical level, but the disease may persist longer or maybe forever.

It is like looking at the tip of an iceberg and assuming it to be where the disease originates. One can keep chipping away at the tip with medicines, but the iceberg will never disappear. As long as the giant remains hidden, it will continue to exist. What constitutes this giant – repressed and suppressed thoughts, strong grudges we keep holding, and unresolved emotions like fear, doubt and attachment – all lead to a vicious cycle of events that not only initiates but also perpetuates the disease. Each thought, each experience of life creates chemicals in the body corresponding to the type of thought. So without mind management, no medicines, no exercise, no diet will have real results. Mind-body management is the crux of health management.

If we want any chronic ailment to get cured, we need a master key that can break both the tip and the larger submerged part of the iceberg. That master key is pranayama – the breathing practices of yoga!

I started the breathing exercises with the primary aim of purifying the blood and cleansing the body of toxins. With regular practice, I started feeling the effects of pranayama not only on the body but also on my mind. Pranayama lifted the veil over my mind and opened the doorway to a clearer vision towards holistic health.

Our relationship with breaths tends to be direct, simple and proportionate as our breaths actually represent the state of our mind – agitated and hot when angry, and calm and gentle with mental relaxation. The dense clouds of unending random thoughts divert the mind from wise thinking.

As the breaths get deeper and slower with regular practice of pranayama, the mental chatter settles down and the mind gets reframed and composed. When a running film slows down, we can see each frame of the picture separately. Similarly, as the breaths slow down, we can see each frame of life more clearly with a third person attitude! This allows our inner wisdom to take over any situation in life, promoting correct decision making and subsequent action.

This is what pranayama does through the practice of slow yet complete breaths. It guided me to the philosophy of living, opening the doors towards healing. How?

• I learnt that I was as vulnerable to illness as any other human being.

• I realised that 'fighting' with my disease would be to set up a pointless no-win battle with myself. Instead, I tried to develop a little detachment and the subsequent objectivity to stand back from what was happening and look at it without getting overwhelmed.

• I learnt to embrace my problem instead of recoiling from it.

• I learnt to love my body instead of hating it.

• I decided to address the cause of my disease by going deeper inwards. Instead of treating the symptoms from outside, I decided to move from inside out so that the healing could be complete.

• During the still moments of pranayama, I was able to

identify the unresolved emotion that had triggered the disease. It taught me that however unfair or undeserved an experience may seem, every experience has a lesson – the more painful the experience, the more important the lesson. Our job is to learn from it, forgiving and forgetting so that we can move on.

• I learnt to acknowledge and accept the realities in my life that I was struggling to change.

• It gave me the inner strength to cope with all that had happened to me. I forgave those who had deeply traumatised my emotional balance and also forgave myself for my reactions. These powerful words helped me substantiate my thought process: The crux of all healing is forgiveness!

The powerful words of Shushruta, one of the strong pillars of the practice of Ayurveda, further enlightened me:

'We don't believe that we have changed. We carry the same mental frame despite body changes. That mental frame retains the disease! We don't let go off that frame and we don't let go off that disease.'

The words of the Zen masters acted as icing on the cake:

'Stop thinking and talking about it and there is nothing you will not be able to know.'

The mental picture of any disease influences the outcome. Prioritising the problem by talking about it now and then further tags it with the individual. I started observing my problems as a third person, and referred to my condition not as a disease but as a 'skin irritation'. I stopped complaining and kept myself busy in the work I loved, so that I had no time to dwell on my condition.

I inserted positive pictures of healthy skin in my mind during the practices of pranayama – a time when the subconscious mind is open to suggestions. I accepted mentally that my condition would improve with time and this is what exactly happened. There is no looking back by Divine Grace!

We can never step in the same river twice. Even modern day physiologists agree that every cell in the body is replaced continuously. Not even one part is the same over time. Our intestines replace themselves every 21 days, every six months our liver replaces itself completely. In fact after seven years, each and every cell of the body has been replaced! So if we can programme our mind to health and wellness, the new cells will accept the call and follow suit. This is wise intelligence and not just information. It's all actually conditioned by the mind.

Any inward discipline and healing requires time and patience. As the natural healing process is slower than that of medication, it requires persistence and commitment. At this stage it is imperative to persevere and not quit, visualising the desired results, knowing that you are on the right track.

Healing often takes a huge turn for the better. Symptoms begin to vanish as if the complete iceberg has been broken! My disease turned out to be a blessing in disguise as it opened my way of thinking, and of handling diseases, to a wider frame. It introduced me to many avenues of healing the body and mind.

I am one of those blessed ones who can boldly say that I am healed; I am cured of a problem that was stubborn, distressing and incapacitating! Having crossed the bridge, I feel it my moral duty to share my healing journey with as many people as possible. Only then am I justifying my identity as a doctor!

Pranayama with an open mind was the key that opened the lock and showed me the way! Many in India and abroad now practice pranayama. Unfortunately, most of us are doing it mechanically like a rigid protocol, without really having tasted its nectar and its positive effects on the mind. All said and done, 75% of the today's ailments originate from the mind and we really have no medicines to work on the mind! We have to learn how to work with our psyche to influence our health positively.

Pranayama offers practical techniques that are very tangible and can be followed by one and all. And why resort to them only in the event of falling sick? Why not now itself so that we can be healthier and happier?

I am reminded of the words of Thomas Hood:

I'm sick of gruel, and the dietetics,
I'm sick of pills and sicker emetics,
I'm sick of pulses, tardiness or quickness,
I'm sick of blood, its thinness and thickness,
In short within a word – I'm sick of sickness.

I present this book for all those who desire to live longer, not as victims of a chronic disease but as masters of their health, with a strong body and mind. This is not an indication to stop medicines because they have their own place where required. Our aim should be to get actively involved in taking care of our own health rather than depending only on our doctor.

'Time is always right to do anything that is right' – *M.L. King*

I aim to share with the reader the very subtle and wide benefits of pranayama not just on the body but also on the mind – only then will we experience holistic health. It is going to be a true adventure as the reader will be amazed, not only by the useful information, but also its scientific validation and practical implications. It is going to be a marvellous discovery for them!

Falling sick is an opportunity to learn humility, build spiritual muscles and to grow beyond norms. The techniques of pranayama and the applications given here are time tested ancient techniques. I am overjoyed to share all these practical and useful discoveries that helped me rediscover my health!

Wishing my readers the best of health,

—Dr. Renu Mahtani M.D.

SECTION I
HOLISTIC HEALTH

Not sickness, but health is the greatest of medical mysteries.
Health is not a condition of matter...
Nor can the material senses bear reliable testimony on the
subject of health.

—*Mark Baker Eddy*

1

What is Health

To keep the body in good health is a duty – otherwise we shall not be able to keep our mind strong and clear.

—BUDDHA

Health is not so much a state, but a force: the power to resist and overcome threats to one's well-being.

—Gregory P. Fields

This is a great error of our day in the treatment of the human being, that the physician separates the soul from the body.

—Plato

Health is the return of the memory of wholeness.

To say that health is the greatest asset in life is an understatement, for it is, in fact, the *only* asset that counts ultimately. All others, including knowledge, intelligence and wealth, have meaning and purpose only when they are associated with a certain degree of physical and mental good health. We also treat health sometimes as if it were a commodity, something that we could buy by visiting a reputed doctor or having innumerable tests done. We may derive some temporary benefit from this, but for any lasting benefits we must understand that **if we want good health, we must deserve it.**

Health is not the absence of disease, but rather an optimum state of body functions. Until recently, the well-being of the body and the mind was regarded as health. According to current thinking however, health is the ability to respond correctly to an ever-changing environment. Our lungs, heart, liver and other organs are all designed to deal with frequent changes. Our health is our capacity to maintain this state of change at the optimum level of efficiency.

The foundation of health is vitality, something that no medical check-up can reveal. Health is not a negative virtue signifying absence of disease. It is something positive, implying an abundance of vitality, vigour and youthfulness. Physical stamina, mental alertness and clarity, and spiritual poise are the blessings of good health.

Does Better Medicine Mean Better Health?

There have been many advances in modern medicine. We now have an enormous amount of information on the body and its working. Tremendous progress has been made in the fields of diagnostics, investigation and early detection of diseases. Life-threatening infectious diseases of the past are under better control with the advent of antibiotics, and surgical treatment has progressed by leaps and bounds. With technological advancements like laproscopic surgery, there are fewer complications, and failure rates have come down significantly. All these advances have considerably increased the average lifespan.

Yet, despite all these advances we have not been able to conquer the major diseases. **Though we live longer, that part of our lifespan which is spent in good health is getting shorter while the period spent suffering from diseases is getting longer.** No one seems to die of only 'old age' any more. Death is due to some disease or the other. Which are these diseases that are multiplying in the wake of advancements everywhere?

   1. **Degenerative diseases:** Chronic immunological diseases affect our quality of life in an adverse way. They are coronary artery disease, cancer, Alzheimer's dementia, arthritis,

rheumatism, diabetes, multiple sclerosis, polymyositis, muscular degeneration, ankylosing spondylitis, vasculitis, and dermatitis. Among the newer names being added are chronic fatigue syndrome, fibromyalgias, and motor neuron disease.

2. **Psychosomatic ailments:** Eighty per cent of the common ailments from which we suffer, such as hypertension, peptic ulcers, colitis, and IBS (Irritable Bowel Syndrome), are a lifelong menace despite medication, which can control but not cure.

3. **Allergies:** Our weakened immune systems have made 'allergy' a common word, frequently bandied about. New infections keep surfacing, and with greater resistance to the widening array of antibiotics.

4. **Heart diseases:** More and more younger people are falling prey to the No.1 killer of the affluent.

5. **Obesity:** Over-eating and bad eating have become a disease of the civilized.

It is disturbing that an overwhelming majority today believes that developing one of these chronic diseases is inevitable. We look to modern medicine and other 'pathies' to save us by providing a cure. Sadly, only after we fall ill do we realize how incomplete the treatments actually are.

We are more concerned with the treatment of disease than with the preservation and promotion of health. Students of medicine are taught a lot about disease, but precious little about health. Why don't we realize that it is far cheaper and easier to remain healthy than to wait for illness to strike and then join in the painful search for remedies? Despite having a normal body weight, normal blood pressure, normal blood sugar and ECG, people are increasingly falling ill. Diseases of the body and the mind are widespread and on the rise because we have neglected holistic health.

Holistic Health

The holistic approach to health is fundamentally different from the modern emphasis on specialization. It believes that diseases and ailments originate deep within, before they appear on the physical and the mental levels, due to a state of imbalance in an otherwise integrated human personality.

It is the human mind that makes or breaks the body and its functions. The mind has tremendous power over the body and is the supreme authority in illness. If we go deeper inwards, we will see that most of the major diseases of the body have their roots in the mind. Seventy-five per cent of diseases are mind-oriented or psychosomatic in nature.

It is surprising to find that there are many people who find life good despite persistent pain. They have found health deeper than on the physical level, and are able to feel well inside themselves, although they know that they are suffering from a disease. This feeling of well-being is the result of an inner, deep and abiding sense that, despite everything, life is good. Research too, documents that this inner health, our own sense of healthiness, is a more accurate predictor of our mortality than an examination by medical personnel and lab tests. Don't people generally live longer than predicted if they are positive-minded with some genuine goals in life?

If we look back on the life we have lived so far, we will realize that we have usually suffered an illness following some setback or disappointment, or when overworked, or under major emotional tension. Even a minor illness has resulted because we had either neglected our diet and exercise, or refrained from giving the body and the mind timely rest. Often we are very tense about something, and ignore our own need to relax and rejuvenate.

During the course of an illness, our field of awareness is usually limited to sensations arising out of the physical body – such as hunger, pain, itching, and so on. With this restricted field of awareness, it is difficult to appreciate how much our thoughts, emotions, likes and dislikes are controlling us. The more we become aware of the different levels, the more we shall realize that there is usually a lack of harmony between our thoughts, words and actions. This leads to chaos, mental speed and stress, and culminates in physical disorders and emotional instabilities. Thus, there is a direct link between stress and illness.

2

Stress and Illness

The mechanism of illness is not the origin of illness. One disease, many cures; many diseases, one cure.

—Chinese Proverb

We are responsible for what we are and whatever we wish ourselves to be, we have the power to make ourselves

—Swami Vivekananda

Live consciously to avoid disease.

We fall prey to illness when we ignore the needs of the body to exercise, eat healthy, and relax; and the needs of the mind to express emotions, and to find a meaning in life. It has been universally observed that illness is more likely to occur after major emotional upsets that suppress the immune system, thus shattering the natural defence mechanisms of the body.

How Does Stress Affect Our Body?

There are physiological mechanisms in our body by which chronic stress and associated emotional states contribute to diseases. A little understanding of the human nervous system in this context will be helpful. Our nervous system is the consequence of many years of evolution. It basically comprises our master computer, the brain; the major cable of the body, our spinal cord; and the network of nerves that links the master computer to the nooks and corners of the body.

Every action that takes place in the body is secondary to its initiation in some part of the brain. For example, the sight and smell of the food of our choice triggers salivation in the mouth after the brain gets information about the food through the sensory nerves coming from the nose and the eyes. The brain then sends signals to the salivary glands in the mouth to produce more saliva. A similar connection of reflex nerve makes us withdraw our hand when we touch something hot. These instantaneous responses of the body to harmful threats form the basis of our survival instinct.

In primitive times, for survival in jungles and less protected surroundings, the brain was tuned to meet external challenges like wild animals and natural threats by triggering a 'fight-or-flight' response in the body. This would enable the body to recruit physiological changes to cope with the demand of either fighting the threat or fleeing from it.

In our day-to-day life too, we have many stressors. When we get angry for any reason, our breathing gets coarse, the heart rate quickens, and the face turns red. Our personality changes and communication becomes aggressive. These changes spontaneously make up the stress response, and are mediated through a well-designed interaction between the nerves and the hormones in the body.

Stress Response

The nervous system is chiefly responsible for the control and integration of a variety of bodily functions. Structurally, the nervous system is made up of the brain, the spinal cord and the network of nerves connecting the master brain to various parts of the body. Functionally, the nervous system can be divided into two parts – the Somatic Nervous System which controls the voluntary actions of the body like walking, writing, and typing; and the Autonomic Nervous System which controls the involuntary actions of the body, that is, actions that are not under our conscious control, such as digestion, excretion, sweating, etc.

Autonomic Nervous System

The Autonomic Nervous System (ANS) is like 'housekeeping' it controls the various involuntary functions of the body. These include breathing, digestion, excretion, peristalsis (bowel movement), sweating, heart beat, metabolic rate, Ph or the acid base balance, and so on.

The ANS operates through its two limbs – the Sympathetic Nervous System (SNS) and the Parasympathetic Nervous System (PNS), responsible for opposing effects on the organs they control. Nerves from both divisions of the ANS supply most of the organs inside the body. By counterbalancing each other's effects, they regulate the functioning of the internal organs and help establish a balanced state called homeostasis. The ANS triggers the body to cope with stress via nerve signals that influence the hormones, which then act on the various organs of the body. Let us see how.

The Sympathetic Nervous System (SNS) is stimulating in character, and prepares us to face emergencies by triggering the fight-or-flight response. This response includes increase in heart rate, blood pressure, and cardiac output; a diversion of blood from the skin to the skeletal muscles; bronchial dilation in the lungs, and metabolic changes for increasing blood sugar levels to meet with the increased demands on the body. This response is vital for gearing up the body to cope with any stressful situation.

The Parasympathetic Nervous System (PNS) works to 'ease-and-release' the effects of stress and to balance the body's response to it. The PNS is soothing and restores normalcy to the system by allowing conservation and restoration of energy. This leads to a normalization of the increased heart rate and blood pressure, facilitation of the digestive processes, and the elimination of waste products. This sympathetic-parasympathetic balance is called homeostasis and is vital to promote well-being and health, and to maintain a balance between extreme anxiety and functional calm.

The Autonomic Nervous System

Structure	Sympathetic Stimulation	Parasympathetic Stimulation
Heart	Heart rate and force increased	Heart rate and force decreased
Lungs Breathing	Increased respiratory rate Ineffective shallow	Slower respiratory rate Deeper breaths
Stomach	Peristalsis reduced (reduced digestion)	Gastric juice secreted; motility increased
Intestines	Motility reduced	Digestion increased
Liver	Increased conversion of glycogen to glucose (to provide more energy) Increased blood sugar levels	
Endocrine glands	Norepinephrine and epinephrine (stress hormones) secreted	

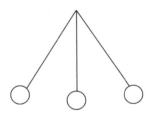

SYMPATHETIC NS	PARASYMPATHETIC NS
Heart rate increased	Heart rate decreased
Blood vessels constricted	Blood vessels relaxed
Increased blood pressure	Reduced arterial pressure
Inhalation	Exhalation
Oxygen transfer into blood stream	Carbon dioxide transfer outside blood

Stress Response in Present Time

Today our challenges and stressors are different from those in primitive times. Instead of wild animals and inhospitable terrain, we have to cope with unending traffic and speeding vehicles, shortage of time and increasing demands, an over-competitive environment, and our struggle for a healthy self-image.

Fighting or fleeing would be socially inappropriate in most cases. So what do we do in the face of such modern stressors? We feel bad and get emotionally disturbed; at a deeper level, we actually tend to override the stressor and suppress the physical reaction to it. Unknowingly we keep suppressing our responses to the unending list of stressors throughout the day. This leads to a negative cumulative effect on the body and manifests as chronic stress, which has not been released.

THE BODY'S HIDDEN MANAGER: THE HYPOTHALAMUS

The Headquarters where the Mind Links with the Body

The hypothalamus is a mini organ buried deep in the brain. Information is transmitted to it from every point in the body, including the sense centres in the brain. It then analyses the information that it has received, decides what measures are to be taken, what changes must be made in the body, and causes the appropriate cells of the body to carry out its decisions.

It has the vital task of ensuring the internal stability of the human body. It performs a number of functions, such as maintaining a stable body temperature, controlling the blood pressure, ensuring a fluid balance, and even, proper sleep-patterns. The expression of emotions such as fear, rage, and anger is partly controlled by the hypothalamus.

One of the most important functions of the hypothalamus is to form a bridge between the hormonal system and the nervous system that control the body. The hypothalamus is the general director of the hormone system as it produces the controlling hormones. It has a special structural and functional relationship with the pituitary gland which is the master gland of the body, as it controls all the other endocrine glands.

Important information passes between the hypothalamus and the pituitary gland through both the nerve fibres (as nerve impulses) and the blood vessels (through the secreted chemicals called hormones). These hormones regulate body processes (metabolism), and control the release of hormones from other endocrine glands like the thyroid, the adrenals and the sex glands (testes or ovaries).

The hypothalamus also establishes the link between the emotional states and the physiological states of the body. It is considered to be associated most directly with the emotions and, through its connection with the ANS, it connects our mental state with all the parts of the body, influencing its various functions.

Chronic stress thus plays an important role in disease genesis by producing an imbalance between the hypothalamus, the nerves, the hormones, and the immune system (defence mechanism) of the body, which work in coordination to maintain the inner balance or homeostasis. Near-constant stressors and internal imbalances can lead to psychosomatic illnesses like high blood pressure, heart disease, ulcers, susceptibility to infections, backaches and even cancer.

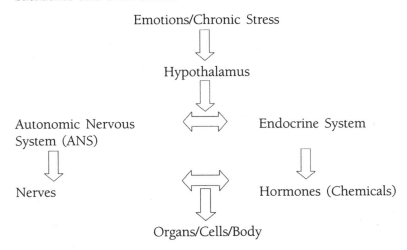

Chronic Stress and Disease Genesis

The world revolves around anxiety and fear of diseases. This fear is worse than the disease, as background anxiety can wreck mental health, leading to earlier precipitation of that disease on the physical level.

We really value good health only when we fall sick. That's when we regret leading an 'unconscious life'. A recent study revealed that a change in lifestyle has resulted in a 60 per cent improvement in the health scenario in the USA. Only 3.4 per cent of the improvement was due to high-tech medical intervention and that too, mostly under emergency situations.

If you fall ill you must take timely help from a good doctor. But that is not all. With an open mind, look back and try to identify and acknowledge any change in lifestyle or thought process, which may be the basic cause for the illness. This will enable you to bring about the necessary changes required for healing and health.

The Body and Beyond

We now need to broaden our vision to understand the holistic human personality and its energy dynamics of which the ancient scriptures of India speak. This will help us understand and appreciate how to achieve holistic health.

Ancient (Vedic) wisdom spoke with authority when it affirmed that the human personality is not just the body. It has various subtler dimensions that make it a thinking, experiencing, and functioning whole. We have only just started using the term 'mind-body medicine'. The Vedas and the Upanishads said that the mind and the body are but two manifestations of the same constituents – the mind as the field of ideas, and the body as the field of atoms and organs. Each helps keep the other working and healthy.

Let us proceed with a binocular-type of understanding to get a full-screen picture of the holistic model of the human personality. This is the beginning of the journey towards health. We shall now adopt a broader vision to see how ancient philosophy meets physiology.

3

Holistic Human Personality

The genius creates, the meditator discovers.

—Osho

He who knows others is wise; he who knows himself is enlightened.

—Lao Tzu

We are more than our body

Our body is the ultimate and the most sophisticated instrument created by nature. The beauty of the body comes from its functions, its innate intelligence, and the life force flowing through it. By itself the body has no identity. It is the integrated whole, the union of the body, breath, and mind – the human personality that tops the list of all possible creations. Indian philosophy has presented a very comprehensive understanding of the human personality as a whole.

One of the most important bases for yoga's truly holistic model of the human system is presented in the *Taitteriya Upanishad.* Known as the 'Panchamaya' or the 'Panchakosha' concept, it enunciates how the five unique aspects of the personality – body, breath, discriminative mind, wisdom and joy – interplay to integrate consciousness and energy into a harmonious and holistic human being, resulting in health and balance.

Panchamaya or the Panchakosha Concept

According to this concept, the human personality has five aspects to it, each integrated and functioning in a composite manner. *Pancha* means five and *kosha* means sheath – the five functioning layers of the holistic human entity.

In the literal sense, koshas can be understood as onion peels, one over the other. This facilitates understanding them on a two-dimensional plane. They are actually different forms of energy that intermingle and interchange. From the gross to the subtle, the Panchakoshas are:

1. The *Annamaya Kosha* or the Physical Body

This is the gross, material aspect of the mind-body complex that is fed, nourished and sustained by *anna* (food), water and air – the gross forms of energy. The various disciplines of modern science have extensively studied, understood, and experimented upon the physical body. Being the quantifiable and the visible aspect, it is given the maximum attention and concern.

Our body cannot sustain itself without the support of the other aspects or koshas. Its existence is even more dependent on *prana* (the life force) and its functions; one can live without food for up to six weeks, without water for six days, without air for six minutes, but life ceases immediately if prana is withdrawn. Can a dead body be revived with oxygen, water and food? The answer is obviously a big 'NO!' because the physical body is non-existent without life energy or prana.

2. The *Pranamaya Kosha* or the Energy Body

Energy moves the physical body: the vital energy responsible for the functioning of the various organs that sustain the internal physiological functions is prana. This field or level is known as the Pranamaya Kosha. This body of energy is subtle yet very powerful. Since it does not have muscles and bones, we have to look at it differently to find its anatomy and physiology. We look at the movement of energy as the breath. Through the breath, we take in prana, which gets distributed to the space between and within the cells and organs.

3.The *Manomaya Kosha* or the Mind Body

The mind or the *manas* is where our everyday thoughts, emotions, sensations, memories, and the power of attention operate. Thoughts are the ultimate manifestation of motion, so the mind is capable of attaining the greatest speed, moving anywhere, anytime. Time and space do not exist as barriers for the mind.

The Manomaya Kosha or the mental sphere is where most present-day maladies originate. With uncontrolled thoughts and emotions it runs riot, forming scars that permeate the body and give rise to disease and illnesses – mental and physical.

Where is the mind located?

There is a centre within us that has the power to decide. On the external front it decides when to stand, stay still or move, and how to respond and react; on the internal front it decides which part of the body needs to do which function. This centre – the mind – is the source of health or disease.

Modern science is still in the process of getting introduced to the human mind. The mind is a subtle, sub-atomic concept present in every human body cell. The body and the mind are not two separate identities but rather an organized whole.

Where is the mind located? In the brain or the heart? This is not a new debate. When we rationalize with logic on issues such as finances, it seems the mind is located in the brain. When we look into the eyes of a newborn baby and get a glimpse of the pure life force there, an expansive feeling of joy fills the heart, as if the mind were there. Actually, each and every cell of the body seems to have the mind, the intelligence, to know what its functions are; for example, damaged skin will regenerate to form skin and not bones, the cells lining the digestive tract know which juice they have to produce, the kidney cells know that they have to filter out the urea and other waste products but absorb the glucose and other nutrients that are also getting filtered out. The list of the miracles of this inner intelligence is unending.

4. The Vijyanamaya Kosha or the Body of Higher Wisdom

We have all experienced the highest wisdom or intuition at some time or the other. The difficult part is getting to trust it. We rely on books and the Internet and other external sources to tell us what to think, to feel and also how to heal ourselves. Rarely do we trust the inner voice, which is always there to guide us, if only we knew how to tune into it.

The Higher Wisdom

The inner voice can be accessed with a calm and clear mind that is free from the chatter of unwanted thoughts. When the mind becomes crystal clear, reflecting what we see without colouring it with its own likes, dislikes and prejudices, we open up to our higher knowledge. This is the experience of the Vijyanamaya Kosha – the body of knowing or wisdom. It discriminates between virtue and vice, truth and untruth, right and wrong.

All discoveries occur as a flash of intuition in the mind of the person who is prepared or tuned-in, who then works to prove it to the world. Albert Einstein was once asked how he had discovered the relationship between matter and energy, and his answer was, 'I meditated and it revealed itself to me.' Meditation creates a state of mental calm and clarity when the body of wisdom speaks out as flashes of intuition.

5. The Anandamaya Kosha or the Body of Bliss

This is the subtlest aspect of our personality: a state of peace, stillness and bliss that we all know exists deep within us. It is the basic ground, which alone remains when feelings and thoughts all become silent. This brings the experience of *ananda* or bliss.

The Interconnectedness

Really speaking, these five koshas, from the gross Annamaya Kosha to the subtlest Anandamaya Kosha, represent a human being's awareness of his or her own existence. Each of these five dimensions is completely and intricately interlinked with all the others. At the same time, they are all completely present everywhere in the system. When one changes, all the others change as well. This interconnectedness is the basis of disease genesis and healing and health as seen in the previous chapters.

Science has looked into Annamaya Kosha, the body. Psychology is looking into Manomaya Kosha, the mind. Parapsychology is making an attempt to look into Vijyanamaya Kosha, but no known 'logy' has made attempts yet to discover the wonders of the Pranamaya Kosha, the area of prana or the life force. This life force is the vital energy which sustains both physiology and psychology, in other words, the functions of the body and the mind.

Let us begin our journey to this less explored area and its functions by first reading about the marvels of prana.

SECTION II
PHILOSOPHY MEETS PHYSIOLOGY

We shall never cease from exploration
And the end of all our exploring
Will be to arrive where we started
And know the place for the first time

—*T. S. Eliot*

4

Prana – Our Energy System and Health

Prana is the life energy by which divinity brings into existence the organic kingdoms and acts on organic structures, as it creates and acts on the universe by means of physical energy.

—Gopi Krishna

Energy crisis – the root cause of our problems

Prana, the Fabric of Creation

When we think of natural energy, we imagine the energy we get from the sun, or perhaps from food. However, there is another form of energy that we develop within the human body. Travelling from cell to cell are pulsating currents of pure electrical energy. These cellular power plants supply vital energy to our organs and muscles to keep our body running efficiently, but we rarely think of this continuous activity within the body. Processes that we take for granted such as breathing, cleansing, elimination, fat control and healing, all depend on these countless cellular energy plants.

Here is something about which we should all seriously think. Our bodies distribute the available energy according to strict priorities. Energy goes first to crucial body functions such as breathing, then to the muscles and the organs, then to digestion, then to cleansing and elimination, and then to healing. As there is only so much energy to go around, most people exist at barely half of their energy potential, the body must pick and choose where it wants the energy to go. That is why half of our body functions are continually being denied.

Fortunately, our body is a lot wiser than we think: it uses its available energy according to the priorities that have been established. If energy is required for some immediate activity such as digestion, it will be directed away from some lesser activity such as cleansing, waste elimination, fat maintenance, or organ and muscle tone, towards the high priority zone.

Owing to this priority system, the activity that requires the most energy, and which frequently gets very little of it, is the natural healing process of the body. Combating disease and infection requires a huge amount of energy but this energy may not be available if our baseline energy levels are low. Our lifestyle and diet burn up so much energy, that our body might not have enough energy left to heal itself.

When our energy supply runs low all the functions of our body are impaired. Digestion, absorption, assimilation, elimination, circulation and respiration become inefficient. All the tissues and fluids of the body become sluggish. The cells are no longer nourished and we feel unwell. Our health declines and we feel sick. This process is called degeneration.

To recharge our energy plants we must provide our body not only with wholesome food and oxygen, but activate a system, a lifestyle, where the vital force that sustains us and our functions is always there for us. This omnipotent energy, which is the basic fabric of the universe, both inside and outside the body, is the life force or prana.

What is Prana?

The term prana comes from the ancient Indian scriptures. Prana is the first energy – *Pra* means first, and *na* is the smallest unit of energy. All aspects and levels of creation manifest out of this first unit of energy. Prana is the primal or atomic beginning of the flow of energy from which emerge all other forms of energy.

Prana is said to be self-existent, infinite and eternal, the one life on which all lives depend, the one existence from which all existences are drawn. Prana is the sum total of all the forces in nature, all the energies that are manifest in the universe.

Prana permeates each individual as well as the universe, at all levels. All that vibrates in the universe is prana — light, heat, sound, magnetism, gravity, electricity, power, vigour, life and vitality. It has been described as a type of complex multi-dimensional energy consisting of a combination of electrical, magnetic, photonic, and thermal energies.

Prana not only spans through the entire spectrum of energy perceivable to man, it is also beyond infrared and ultraviolet energy. It exists in the subtlest form, which has not yet been quantified by existing scientific tools and methodologies.

Prana is more minute than an atom, for it is within every atom as its in-dwelling life. There is nothing so huge that it can over-stretch prana; there is nothing so tiny that it can escape prana. It has no form, no colour, no outline; but all forms draw their beauty from it, all colours are portions of its white light, all outlines are expressions of it.

This 'vital force' may sound a little mystical, since it cannot be measured with conventional scientific equipment. Yet in our daily language we often refer to our energy level, which is high at certain times and low at others. Our experience validates the concept of energy even though we cannot measure it.

The working of prana is seen in the systolic and diastolic actions of the pumping heart; in the inhalations and exhalations of respiration; in the digestion and absorption of food; in the excretion of urine and faeces; in the manufacturing of gastric juices, bile, saliva, chyle, and semen; in the closing and opening of the eyelids; and in walking, talking, thinking, reasoning and feeling. When the prana withdraws from the body, it dies. No oxygen, saline or glucose drip, or technology can revive it.

Prana is not just our physical energy but also the subtler mental energy where the mind gathers information; the intellectual energy where information is examined and filtered. It also acts as sexual energy to procreate and transform the single fertilized cell to a well-differentiated intellectual being that is capable of independent existence. Prana is our spiritual energy and the omnipresent cosmic energy.

The stronger the life force in us, the better we look and feel; the associated clarity of mind makes decisions easier, and emotions find their correct place, bringing us fulfilment in the smallest things we do. Without prana we would be decaying corpses with no ability to see, move or hear.

Pranic energy is available in negative ions, oxygen, ozone, and solar radiation, and for human beings the media is the breath. By mastering prana one can master the mind. The science of controlling the prana is called pranayama.

Forms of Prana

Simply put, prana is 'that which supports the physiology of the body'. It is comparable to the role electricity plays in electronic machinery. Without electricity, nothing in the machine works, but when electricity is present, the machine can perform its functions. Prana gets transformed into various powers in the body for carrying out different functions. This vital energy has five major functional aspects that are felt to be more active in specific regions of the body. These functional aspects of prana have been given different names according to the bodily functions with which they correspond.

Prana Prana: That which enters the body is called prana, and this corresponds to the functions in the chest region. Since the body constantly needs energy for all its activities, it is necessary to replenish it by bringing in energy from outside the body. The term prana prana refers to all the happenings responsible for sustaining and continuing the life process – the heart and the lungs.

Udana Prana: It corresponds to the head and the neck regions, and is responsible for all the higher functions of speech, expression, comprehension and communication.

Samana Prana: Samana means 'balanced' or 'equal'. Samana prana is situated in the central region of the body between the navel and the rib cage. It controls the digestive organs and their secretions, and is responsible for digestion and assimilation of nutrients.

Apana Prana: It corresponds to the lower abdomen region, and the pelvic region between the navel and the perineum. It controls the function of elimination – the kidneys, the bowels, the bladder, the excretory and the reproductive organs. It is responsible for the expulsion of gas, urine, faeces, and the foetus at the time of birth, and hence, it has a downward moving force.

Vyana Prana: It corresponds to the distribution of energy to all areas of the body, and pervades the entire body. It regulates and coordinates all the muscular movements in the body through the nervous system.

The Interplay – Prana and Apana

Apana refers not only to the activities of elimination occurring in the lower part of the body, but also to the energy required for it. So, although apana is needed as pranic energy, when left in the body as refuse, it prevents prana from developing.

How Much Prana Do I Need?

All forms of prana are necessary but they need to be in a state of balance with each other. For good health, the goal is to increase prana prana, and reduce apana prana to the minimum. Apana as waste matter accumulates due to various factors, many of which are in our control. The practice of yoga can reduce these impurities.

The toxic impurities, apana, leave the body through the lungs. During inhalation prana enters the body to meet apana, while during exhalation the apana within the body moves out. When we hold our breath after inhalation, prana moves towards apana, and vice versa. When we are short of breath, cannot hold our breath, or cannot exhale slowly, it is because we have more apana; less apana in the body results in breathing with good control.

The yogic science of pranayama trains the body to remove apana, so that prana can find more room within. It creates the conditions in which prana may enter the body and permeate it.

Why Do We Need More Prana?

Prana is the sustaining principle of life – the upholder of both the structure and the functions of the body. It is the inspirer of all the senses, the conveyor of all the sensory and motor stimuli, the controller and conductor of the mind. Thus more prana will vitalize all functions of the body and the mind, immunity, healing and the essence of life.

Scientific Proof

1. Prana and its forms were photographed about five decades ago through Kirlian photography. According to some scientists, prana is cloud-like, and has electromagnetic energy. The sub-divisions of prana have ionic fields of varying densities. Clairvoyants can see prana as swirling clouds of different shades and colours.

2. Prana has been referred to as the biofield – a massless field that surrounds and permeates living bodies. Scientists have proved the existence of the pranic body and biofields with the help of innovative equipment.

- At the University of California, Los Angeles, kinesiologist Valerie Hunt and her associates found electronic evidence of the biofield. This was done with the use of electromyographic equipment that measures the steady, low voltage waveforms that represent electrical activity in the muscles.

- Dr. Hiroshi Motoyama, president of the International

Association for Religion and Parapsychology, has created an apparatus for measuring the functions of the meridians and the corresponding internal organs. This machine is able to measure minute changes in nervous system activity in the order of one to ten microseconds.

3. Prana has been equated with the negatively charged ions present in the environment. A predominance of these negative ions has been observed to have a stimulating and vitalizing effect on the body, whereas a predominance of positive ions depresses the system. In a study, when people were exposed to positive ions, they became lethargic, and irritable, and developed respiratory defects and headaches. When the negative ions were increased, the whole system got reactivated and energized.

Things can be defined scientifically because science is looking for something physical and measurable, whereas there are myriad things in existence that are non-physical and non-quantifiable. How can one measure infinity? If infinity can be measured with an instrument, then it is not infinity. Prana is one such miracle – too vast and too subtle to be measured.

Just as electricity is the unseen basis for heat and light, prana is the base of all the physiological and psychological functions in our body. Prana is the green colour of the grass and the plants. It is the hardness of stone. It is the softness of cotton. It is the life force of a human being. Call it what you wish, because tradition says that everything in this world is prana, the force of life. Everything vibrates with that force, that pulsation of life, from the so-called inanimate to the animate forms. This prana enjoys a very special place!

Nadis – the Network

The pranic energy that governs all the functions in the body uses specific channels to move. These channels are known as *nadis*. The word nadi means 'river' or 'channel'. These nadis are the flowing currents of energy through which prana is able to get to different areas in the system. There is an intricate network of nadis all over the body, estimated at well over 72,000 by ancient yogis; they are related, but not equivalent, to the nerves. We can compare nadis to the pathways in the air that aircraft have to follow. In the same way, prana follows specific pathways that cannot be shown in material form. They can, however, be felt in the form of subtle inner sensations. Nadis are the equivalent of the energy meridian in the acupuncture system.

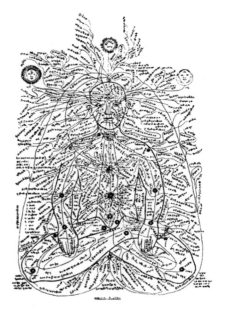

Pranayama

Among the thousands of nadis there are three very powerful energy channels which, when sufficiently purified, can promote the development of the human being on all three planes – physical, mental and spiritual, allowing us to reach higher levels of consciousness. These channels are Ida, Pingala and Sushumna.

The configuration of these three major nadis can be seen in books on yoga. Amazingly, they are represented prominently in the figure of Caduceus from ancient Greece. The image of

Caduceus is today the universal symbol of medicine. The central rod is symbolic of the spinal canal through which the central nadi or the Sushumna runs. The Ida and the Pingala nadis are represented in the Caduceus by the two entwined snakes with their origins at the spinal base, moving up in a spiral manner, crossing at points, which are symbolic of the *chakras* or the primary energy centres in the body.

Caduceus

The knowledge of the ancient yogis has opened a whole vista of exciting studies, especially in the West. This presents a new and comprehensive view of the mind-body dynamics and the physiological states. Scientific studies are coming to an understanding that both the Ida and the Pingala nadis define certain physiological states within us.

The Ida nadi originates from the left side of the base of the spine and after transversing upwards, in a spiral, it reaches the roof of the left nostril. It controls all the activities that are anabolic or constructive in nature, activities that conserve energy and give a cooling effect to the body.

The Pingala nadi rises from the right side of the base of the spine, and after transversing upwards, reaches the roof of the right nostril. It controls the activities of the body that consume energy and generate heat in the body.

Thus the Ida and the Pingala nadis have opposite functions. What one can accelerate, the other can slow down. According to the ancient seers when both Ida and Pingala become active simultaneously, the Sushumna nadi, which is located right in the centre of the spine, gets stimulated. When it gets active, mental and physical energy patterns become even and rhythmic, leading to inner harmony.

Man's major task is the regulation of 'the pairs of opposites'. When the negative and the positive forces of the body, which are expressed via the Ida and Pingala nerve routes, are equilibrated, the forces can ascend and descend by the central channel to and from the brain, passing through the centres up the spine without hindrance.

Wherever energy becomes blocked or cannot flow efficiently for some reason, the normal functioning of the different body parts becomes disrupted and if this lasts for a longer time, diseases can emerge. Techniques to balance the breaths also balance the flow of energy in the nadis and throughout the body, resulting in inner harmony and good health. Pranayama techniques act to purify the nadis including these three main energy channels.

Yogis discovered a long time ago that breathing through the left nostril stimulates the Ida *nadi* or the 'moon channel' (connected with the Parasympathetic Nervous System). Breathing through the right nostril stimulates the Pingala nadi or the 'sun channel' (connected with Sympathetic Nervous System). By balancing the functioning of both nadis (that is, both aspects of the Autonomic Nervous System), we can stimulate the main energy channel called Sushumna and harmonise the activity of the nervous system as a whole

Physical Correlates

The Sympathetic Nervous System (SNS) and the Parasympathetic Nervous System (PNS) – the two wings of the Autonomic Nervous System which governs the involuntary functions of the body (Refer Chapter 3), are hypothesised to be the physical and functional manifests of the Pingala and the Ida nadis. When their functioning is balanced, there is homeostasis or balance in the bodily functions.

The Ida (moon) nadi corresponds with the state of the nervous system and energetics that are identified with the airflow dominating through the left nostril, while the Pingala (sun) nadi is associated with the airflow dominating the right nostril.

When airflow dominates through the right nostril, it is found to co-relate with greater activity in the left brain hemisphere (the Pingala state). When airflow dominates through the left nostril, it co-relates to greater cerebral activity in the right brain hemisphere (the Ida state).

The right cerebral hemisphere has been found to assume responsibility for the artistic, intuitive, spatial and holistic side, which function also belongs to the Ida nadi. The left side of the brain has centres for verbal communication, hearing, reading, talking and writing, and is responsible for our logical, rational and analytical faculties. This is also the function of the Pingala nadi. Thus, the right side of the brain is activated when the left nostril is flowing, and the left side of the brain is activated when the right nostril is flowing.

This interrelation between our breaths, nasal dominance and body-brain functions has been discussed a little more in detail in Chapters 17 and 18. Let us now understand the chakras and their influence on our personality and health. Chakras could be called junction points in the body where the energy or prana gets concentrated to interact with the endocrine or the hormone secreting system and the nervous system to influence our psycho-physiological functions.

5

Chakras – The Energy Hubs

The greatest deception men suffer is from their opinion.

—Leonardo da Vinci

In all chaos there is a cosmos, in all disorder, a secret order.

—Carl Jung

Where consciousness links with the body

Man is a living organism, but where is the life, the consciousness, integrated within the various parts of the body? Philosophically, our existence is the union of two primal forces – consciousness and vital energy that is, prana. Without consciousness, the omnipresent energy cannot manifest its dynamic nature.

Many years ago, yogis devised a practical and systemic view of energy and consciousness that involved seven discreet levels. Each level was related to what yogis called the chakras, or centres of energy. The pranic network is fuelled by chakras that are high-powered vortices of energy. They receive the cosmic prana and act as transformers so that it can be used by the various organs and parts of the body.

When these energy centres are out of harmony, the vital force is unable to circulate freely, leading to distress, diseases and lack of mind-body integrity. Good health requires free flow of prana in the body, and proper balance between the energy hubs or chakras.

Each chakra is instrumental in determining the personality structure, the behaviour and the level of awareness of an individual. This depends, of course, on the amount of energy and activity in individual chakras.

A balance is required between the chakras. All are equally important, but every individual has only one chakra that dominates in establishing his personality. As time goes by however, this chakra may lose its dominance and some other may gain importance, depending on the personality change that occurs in the individual. Many diseases also result from imbalances in these centres.

Correlates in the Body

Prominent research scientists – Dr. David S. Khalsa from the University of California, San Diego, and Dr. Hiroshi Motoyama from Japan – who have integrated eastern sciences with western medicine, explain chakras as energy plexuses in the human body, and speak of the flow of energy through them using the language of a quantum scientist.

The primal force manifests itself in the physical body through the neuro-endocrine system: the nervous system and the endocrine system are the prime regulators. If either of these two fails, the body gets jeopardized. The nervous system (through the wide network of nerves) and the endocrine system (through chemical regulators called hormones coming from the ductless glands in the body) exert control over all our physical, mental, behavioural and emotional functions.

Each chakra or energy centre has a physiological correlate in the body, thought by some to correspond to the autonomic nerve plexuses and an endocrine gland, where different energies interact.

The endocrine glands are the intercommunicating transformers between the subtle and the gross. They translate the code of the intangible spiritual forces into a form of crude power, which can work on the gross physical body through the nervous system. The sensory nerves are the media of consciousness, carrying its impulses, while the motor nerves are the media of vital energy manifesting itself.

The sympathetic system, as the thoracolumbar outflow (arising from that part of the spinal cord which is in the thorax or the chest, and the lower back or the lumbar region), and the parasympathetic system as the craniosacral outflow (cranial means from the brain and sacral from the tail bone region or the tail of the spinal cord) of nerves, create the network of plexuses which link physiologically with the endocrine system.

Therefore, chakras could be considered the junction points between consciousness and physiology. These energy centres govern the core emotional and physical functions of the body. They could be considered the cosmic network hubs, and the nadis as the multi-gigabyte-per-second optical fibre wiring.

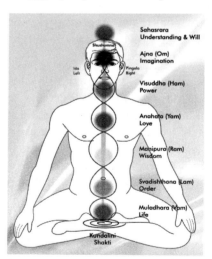

The Chakra System – States of Consciousness

The first chakra – the Muladhara, Base, or Root Chakra:
related to instinct, security, survival and basic human

potentiality. This centre is located in the region between the genitals and the anus. Although no endocrine organ is present here, it is said to relate to the inner adrenal glands – the adrenal medulla – responsible for the fight-and-flight response when survival is under threat. In this region is located a muscle that controls ejaculation in the sexual act. A parallel is drawn between the sperm cell and the ovum, where the genetic code lies coiled.

The Muladhara, or Root, Chakra is the lowest of the chakras and is the seat of primal energy. The consciousness of an individual who lives mainly in the first chakra is concerned primarily with survival. His action and values are based solely on the need to survive. Imbalances here can lead to a rigid and stubborn mentality. This chakra is physiologically related to the area of the rectum – the sacro coccygeal plexus of nerves.

The second chakra – the Swadhisthana or Sacral Chakra: located in the groin, and related to base emotions, sexuality and creativity. This chakra corresponds to the testicles or the ovaries, which produce the various sex hormones involved in the reproductive cycle, and can cause dramatic mood swings. The Swadhisthana Chakra is related to the sex organs (sacral plexus). A balanced sacral chakra helps establish a creative and expressive mentality. Over-activity in this chakra however, leads to sexual neurosis. One needs to develop will-power in order to go beyond this centre. It is located at the base of the spine at the level of the tail bone and the pubis.

The third chakra – the Manipura or Solar Plexus Chakra: related to the transition from the base to the higher emotions, energy, assimilation and digestion, and corresponding to the roles played by the pancreas and the outer adrenal glands – the adrenal cortex. These play an important role in digestion, the conversion of food matter into energy for the body. The Manipura Chakra is located at the level of the navel. This is the seat of power (solar plexus). It also represents vitality, dynamism, ego and intellect. When balanced, it is the source of physical well-being, but when imbalanced, it leads to a range of illnesses, a weak character, poor will-power and drive. The 'me' mentality prevails to the exclusion of others.

These three levels of consciousness prevail throughout the animal kingdom. Much of society's ills are a result of an imbalance in these chakras. The biggest step in human development is an ascent from this level of consciousness to a higher level via the other four chakras.

The fourth chakra – the Anahata or Heart Chakra: related to higher emotion, compassion, love, equilibrium, and well-being. It is related to the thymus, located in the chest. This organ is part of the immune system as well the endocrine system. It produces T cells responsible for fighting disease, and is adversely affected by stress. The Anahata Chakra, or the heart centre (cardiac plexus), embraces the human element of compassion, the attitude of giving and nurturing. Universal love is born through activity in this centre. It is considered to be the first level of higher consciousness, where one can experience true awareness. A person with a developed Anahata Chakra is generally very sensitive to the feelings of others, and is free of selfishness and emotional attachment. On the other hand, when the Heart Chakra is not awakened, greed, selfishness and ego dominate.

The fifth chakra – the Vishuddha or Throat Chakra: related to communication and growth, the latter being a form of expression. This chakra is parallel to the thyroid, a gland in the throat that produces the thyroid hormone, which is responsible for growth and maturation. It is also called the throat centre or the laryngeal plexus. This is the centre for communication through expression located at the level of the throat pit. When active, this centre enables a person to be a good speaker and even a blunt one. When blocked, the person feels stifled and is less truthful and direct in his attitude.

The quality of higher consciousness that manifests itself in this centre is that of clairvoyance. The person is able to receive thought vibrations from other people. It is also the centre for receiving sound vibrations. Thus the sense of hearing is heightened through the ears as well as the mind.

The sixth chakra – the Ajna Chakra or the Third Eye: linked to the pineal gland. Ajna is the chakra of time and awareness, and of light. The pineal gland is a light-sensitive gland that produces the hormone melatonin, which regulates the instincts of falling asleep and awakening. Melatonin is also the anti-aging hormone. The Ajna Chakra is the commanding or the monitoring centre. It is the point where the three major nadis (the Ida, the Pingala and the Sushumna) meet.

This centre is also known as theThird Eye. It is the centre of intuition and wisdom, through which direct, mind-to-mind communication takes place. It allows both sides of the coin to be seen, beyond the polarities of right and wrong. This centre is therefore, responsible for intuition and clairvoyant abilities. It is located at the top of the spinal cord, mid-brain. It corresponds to the pineal gland, which is particularly active in children. However, this begins to decay at the time of puberty. The trigger point for the chakra is at the centre of the eyebrows. This is an important focal point for practising meditation and visualization.

The seventh chakra – the Sahasrara or Crown Chakra: the chakra of consciousness, the master chakra that controls all the others. Its role is very similar to that of the pituitary gland, which secretes hormones to control the rest of the endocrine system, and also connects to the central nervous system via the hypothalamus. The thalamus has a key role in the physical basis of consciousness.

The Sahasrara Chakra is the centre for pure thoughts and saintly intelligence. Here, actions are based on concern for the highest good for all. This centre is also known as the thousand-petalled lotus. It is the seat of Universal consciousness, the doorway through which one is connected with the prana, which moves upward and reaches the highest point. It is located at the crown of the head and is related to the pineal gland and the cerebral cortex.

6

Health is a Mental Habit

Human pain is always some form of non-acceptance, some form of unconscious resistance to what is.

—Eckhardt Tolle

To the mind that is still, the whole universe surrenders.

—Lao Tzu

Mind prana imbalance leads to diseases.

With the background understanding of the holistic human personality where body, breath and mind are interrelated, let us understand disease genesis at a level where matter meets energy.

In modern medicine, disease is generally considered a result of external causes. Even in the face of infections, the modern hypothesis of disease genesis refers to germs that attack the body, and have to be killed with powerful drugs. Sometimes the damaged part of the body has to be surgically removed. Such 'cures' do nothing to correct the internal imbalances and toxicity that have allowed the disease to occur in the first place. As a result, the disease recurs, over and over again and in different forms, in different parts of the body. This traps the affected person in a vicious cycle of toxic drugs that further deplete energy, leading to further degeneration and disease.

The ancient physicians of India and the oriental countries

described the root cause of disease not as an external attack by germs, but an internal degeneration and toxicity that create imbalances and permit external attacks. Many physicians from European countries too, believed this.

Role of Bio-magnetism or Prana in Health and Disease

Every cell in the body is a laboratory in itself – a complete structure with its own magnetic, electrical and chemical functions. Through its bio-magnetic function it draws what it needs from the running system and eliminates what it does not need. The millions of cells in the body are held together by polar attraction and that is how the body stays in one piece. And what produces this polar bond?

Tiny particles of life force circulate in and around every cell. They keep rotating, and this rotation produces a bio-magnetic field of energy. This bio-magnetism could be called 'crystallized prana': it is the vital force that fuels all the metabolic functions of the body. A small portion of this wave is released through our sense organs – ears, eyes, nose and skin – after getting converted into sound, light, smell and pressure, respectively. This bio-magnetism maintains inner order and integration in the body.

A major portion of this bio-magnetic energy is used up by the body for its metabolic routine – digestion, elimination, repair and maintenance. According to Ayurveda, this bio-magnetic energy transforms digested food into body components, the sequence being: food – juices – blood – flesh – fat – bone – marrow – sexual vital fluid. The remaining bio-magnetic energy goes to the mind to enable it to feel, understand, comprehend, learn, experience and reflect. If the level of this bio-magnetic energy comes down, the result is first, a short supply to the mind leading to lethargy, lack of alertness and deranged mental functions.

Disease genesis occurs when the bio-magnetic energy is in constant short supply. If the energy flowing through the body gets obstructed at some point, it stagnates and the polarity of the cells gets disrupted. The blocked energy does the job of creating a 'short circuit' in the system and starts 'burning' cells. If this involves a small area it gives rise to pain; if it extends over a larger area or for a longer duration it then manifests as disease. Total exhaustion of the bio-magnetic energy is death.

Bio-magnetic Energy/Prana and Our Mind

Very few realize that disease comes through inaction of the life force within, due to scarcity and imbalance in the levels of the bio-magnetic energy, prana, in the body. And why do we get low in the content of prana in our system? This happens mainly due to faulty and ineffective breathing habits, chronic stress and its effect on our mind.

Our mind has tremendous power over the body, and is the supreme authority in illness. There is no major disease of the body that does not have its roots in the mind. In fact our mind, our breaths, our energy levels and prana, are all interrelated. Our state of mind is closely linked to the quality of prana or the energy within. The more prana a person has, the more content and balanced he or she will be. The more disturbed a person is, the more the prana that gets dissipated and lost. When we feel unwell, restless and confused, the quality of prana and its density within the body are reduced. Too little prana in the body manifests itself as a lack of drive, listlessness, and depression. We suffer from physical ailments too, when prana is lacking in the body.

Wrong Attitude Causes Suffering

Thus, our beliefs and attitude to life contribute to our illness. A growing body of data links negative and positive emotional states to wellness or illness. The significance of negative feeling as the leading risk factor for major diseases has been established. Our thoughts, sentiments, emotions, feelings, passions, likes and dislikes, all create physiological changes in the body.

Psychosomatic illnesses start in the mind before showing up in the body. Therefore, we ourselves participate in our health or illness. We play an active role in creating our own level of health through our feelings, emotions, beliefs, attitude towards life, and lifestyle.

Illnesses keep surfacing despite normal medical reports. Deep down, we know that there's more to health than what we are doing and the way we are living presently. A good diet and healthy eating habits, exercise and necessary medicines help make us feel better, but the sickness persists, although, maybe, with less intensity. With all the demands, responsibilities and pressures of today's fast-paced life, we sometimes feel that the turmoil, pain, hurt and disease will never end. And they never will, as long as the roots of the disease remain in the mind

To experience health, we have to work on all levels – body, breath and mind – and get actively involved in creating health.

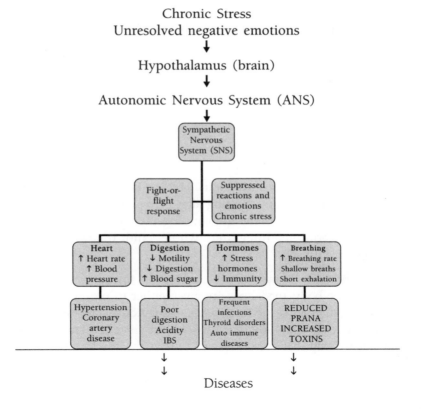

Chronic Stress
Unresolved negative emotions
↓
Hypothalamus (brain)
↓
Autonomic Nervous System (ANS)
↓

| Sympathetic Nervous System (SNS) |

| Fight-or-flight response | Suppressed reactions and emotions Chronic stress |

| Heart ↑ Heart rate ↑ Blood pressure | Digestion ↓ Motility ↓ Digestion ↑ Blood sugar | Hormones ↑ Stress hormones ↓ Immunity | Breathing ↑ Breathing rate Shallow breaths Short exhalation |

| Hypertension Coronary artery disease | Poor digestion Acidity IBS | Frequent infections Thyroid disorders Auto immune diseases | REDUCED PRANA INCREASED TOXINS |

↓   ↓
↓   ↓
Diseases

7

Active Healing – Restoring Prana

Natural forces within us are the healers of disease.

—Hippocrates

The true mystery of the world is the visible, not the invisible.

—Oscar Wilde

The greatest leverage for healing is found at the subtlest levels of function.

—Rudolph Theodore

Be the doer and not the victim.

Vibrant glowing health is our natural state of being, and healing is a biological process of the body. Healing is defined literally as 'making whole or sound, uniting after being cut or broken'. At a deeper level, healing is the drawing together of body and mind into a harmonious integrated whole, and renewal of our connection with life.

In fact, the body knows how to heal itself. In the event of any injury to the body, medicines are given either to prevent or treat secondary infections, or to alleviate pain. Actual healing of the wound occurs innately because of the mechanisms in an intelligent body that recruit special cells at the site to repair and normalize.

We all have inner resources: the forces within us are always at work to help heal the body. We become aware of this phenomenon only when we are undergoing some major illness or life experience. This self-healing is not quackery; it is entirely based on common sense and wisdom. Recent scientific research has powered the idea that self-healing must complement conventional medical treatment strategies.

Healing Is Holistic

Medical science has invested a lot of time and money in finding cures for various diseases. A cure involves the human system in its physical aspect. Some diseases do get cured – such as infections or injuries due to external reasons like bacteria, viruses, and accidents. For various chronic diseases, medicines can keep the symptoms under control but cannot really cure them completely. The word 'cure' has a limited meaning for cancer where getting 'cured' means surviving for a maximum of five years with treatment.

Healing has a wider spectrum as it is essentially holistic in nature, and goes deeper than just the body. The lack of a definitive cure for an illness does not mean that there can be no healing for the individual. True healing actually means transcendence or going beyond the norms. It means rising above fixed beliefs about our problems and reaching new levels of achievement.

Healing should not be measured by the things accomplished, but by our increasing understanding, ability, and closeness to reality. It means finding what we really want, which is not just outward things, but inner peace of mind, balance, joy and self-understanding.

When such healing occurs, mental, emotional and physical suffering is alleviated, and the quality of life improves. Let me give you an example: a patient of mine, a young alcoholic boy, barely twenty years of age, spent most of his time doing nothing. I urged him to join our yoga classes and chose a batch where he would find people of his age. After a few days of reluctant attendance, I noticed that he was chanting the *shlokas* and *mantras* with zeal and involvement. He became so interested in chanting that he took Sanskrit classes and music lessons. This was healing in the true sense – a change in mind, attitude and perception. This healing has to come from within.

Healing Chronic and 'Incurable' Diseases

Staying healthy in the face of incurable and chronic diseases is not only a matter of taking medicines and vitamins, having healthy eating habits, and exercising properly. The most important and crucial thing is to keep a healthy state of mind. Only then can one experience healing. For true physical, emotional and spiritual health, it is as important to eliminate the impurities of emotional wounds as it is to eliminate waste matter from the body. Awareness, harmony, mental clarity and inner balance are the principal factors in establishing a state of balance in man.

'Attitude' is the most important factor in healing incurable diseases. Many people actually want to remain unhappy, dissatisfied, sad, miserable and unhealthy. Their negative personality traits develop into a tendency to attract diseases. They then assume that healing is something done to them, and their job is just to go to a doctor, who will then heal them. It is true to a certain degree but it is not the whole story. Rather than just receive treatment passively, the individual has to play an active role in this journey towards health.

Active Healing

Active healing means getting actively involved in making ourselves physically, mentally, emotionally and spiritually whole. This does not mean minimizing or negating the role of the doctor involved in the treatment. It involves expanding our vision about ourselves as a mind-body complex, and acknowledging the role of our thoughts and emotions in our health.

A person seeking active healing takes responsibility for his health and is willing to embrace lifestyle changes. Along with medical treatment, he modifies his lifestyle, analysing existing habits and thought-patterns, and replacing some with healthier ones. This involves taking charge of how we live, eat, and think, and also the choice of doctor, among other factors. It might mean delaying surgery and opting for herbal remedies and meditation, or supplementing allopathic medicines as required. Active healing means that we make these decisions, monitor our progress, and alter our choices accordingly.

One does not have to try to achieve the impossible or follow extreme restrictions. The idea is to decide what is best for us and take the responsibility for implementing changes according to our individual capacity. Recent investigations prove that within each individual lies the key to relief from mental, physical, psychological, and emotional disorders.

It is never too late to adopt a new attitude towards health. A healthy lifestyle is easy to follow as it boosts confidence and allays fear and misery. A 'pill for every ill' is not the only answer. The time for openness has come: to explore, get involved with active participation, and rediscover health. We need a balanced mental state to take responsibility, and make wise decisions to mobilize our own resources to heal the body and the mind.

The 'illness concept' and the prevailing fear of diseases result in more illness. This has to be replaced by a 'wellness concept' where health is a birthright, and one actively participates in one's own health by adopting a conscious lifestyle.

What Happens in Healing

Healing is not a miracle. It is simply working with energy that comes from cosmic energy. No one can deny that we all are a part of the cosmic energy which has not only created us, but also nourishes and sustains us, keeping us alive, healthy and energized. Cosmic energy is important for sustenance of life, while food and oxygen are the fuels.

Unlike other forms of energy that are tangible and quantifiable –

like light, heat and electric energy—cosmic energy is intangible and immeasurable. But all said and done, it is the intangible that drives the tangible: cosmic energy drives all our physical, emotional and mental functions. Just as our body cannot function without cosmic energy, the mind too, cannot think and work in its absence.

To heal the body and the mind, we basically need more cosmic energy – prana. This extra energy will then pep up the natural healing mechanisms of the body, and bring the neuro-metabolic derangements into order. It will also help build the awareness, mental clarity and inner balance that is greatly required in our fast-paced life. This mental state will then lead us towards making the correct decisions in all respects towards better health.

Thus, healing is restoring the natural flow of prana. Basically, at the root level, medicines, massage and tonics help stimulate the cells in such a way that the life energy, prana, is induced to return and resume its work of maintenance and repair. But at times, they are not enough to adequately restore the energy balance. Thus, to enjoy a better state of health we need:

• A tool to handle the mind because, by changing the mind, diseases can be changed to 'eases'.

• A tool to get more prana in the body

Holistic Approach to Health through a Way of Living Called Yoga

For centuries man has been aware of an inner power that can be tapped to accelerate body healing and improve the state of mental health. Way back in time, the East offered the techniques and philosophy of a 'way of living' called yoga, and the West has made commendable efforts to scientifically prove its tenets.

Our forefathers who practised the ancient system of yoga were open-minded scientists and practical philosophers. They emphasized the importance of holistic health, because they understood that, by balancing the physical, the mental and the spiritual planes of existence, we become better equipped to handle our health.

The yogic approach to health is not just holistic, but also simple, practical, logical and effective. In addition to the biological (physical) and the physiological (functional) aspects of health, it also addresses the psychological and the philosophical concepts. This scientific discipline has been perfected over millennia. That it works has been proven and validated by people from many disciplines.

This discipline lays emphasis on balance and inner harmony — *yuktaaahaar* and *vihaar* — right eating, right breathing and right living. It is possible to gain control over our life and health by understanding our capacities and learning how to regulate our dietary habits, external activities, breathing habits, and thinking process. This is holistic health.

Power of Pranayama

Yoga stands apart as a unique system of health because it aims to correct the energy dynamics of the body and the mind through the lore of techniques that it has, particularly pranayama

Yoga techniques of pranayama, that is, the control and expansion of cosmic energy using the breath, help the individual to get more cosmic energy to heal the physical body and to attain awareness and harmony. The basic approach of the ancient science of pranayama is holistic, as are the results.

This tool is our breath — the vital breath that is a physiological reality! With simple techniques of breath-management, we can attain better physical, emotional and psychological health. Breath-management helps our life energy to resume its internal healing activities, and streamlines our mind towards harmony and balance.

Why the Breath?

Our body and mind are very closely interconnected. Physical phenomena reflect our state of mind, and the state of mind is expressed in physical phenomena. Breath is the bridge between the body and the mind, and it gets instantaneously affected by the two. It is a two-way street. The way we breathe is an indicator of the level of emotional and physical well-being that we are experiencing at that moment. Breath is the physical counterpart of the mind, hence breathing is also known as 'mind in action'.

There is a correlation between our breath and our mind. Whatever happens in the mind influences the breath. The rate and depth of our breath changes depending on our mental state. When we are excited the breath becomes quicker, and when we are calm and relaxed, it becomes quieter. Any activity that requires total concentration will also control our breath. For example, while threading a needle, our breath stops for a moment; the thought process also stops for a few seconds as the mind is engaged.

When the mental state has a strong influence on our breath, can we not manipulate our breath to influence the mind? Yes, we can voluntarily tackle our mind and our emotions through the breath and the life force that connects us all, and that is the science of pranayama.

Through pranayama—the science of the control of prana or the life force—one uses the breath to manage the amount, flow and distribution of energy to both the body and the mind. If we can manage the breath, we can manage both the body and the mind. This is the aim of this book—breath-management for both body-management and mind- management.

Heal the breath and heal the body and the mind!

As we breathe, so shall we live! Breath, being the carrier of the vital force within us, is life itself. To build a harmonious relationship with life, understanding the breath and its ways of working will be useful and health-promoting. Our breath is actually our constant and unfailing friend, and the way we breathe points to the way we live.

Basic Principles of Healing

• Healing is the natural order of life.

• There is an underlying, in-dwelling, healing force in all of us.

• Refusal to be healed is through one's own will, and is counter to the natural system of health.

• As we open our mind to healing, many powerful changes can be expected.

• It is quite safe to open ourselves to the greater healing force.

• As we move towards healing, we move towards Divinity.

SECTION III
BREATH-WORK

Teach me, O God, not to torture myself,
not to make a martyr of myself
through stifling reflection, but rather teach
me to breathe deeply in faith.

—*Kierkegaard*

We are made of stardust, of the cosmos,
of the stuff of where we come from.

—*Carl Sagan*

8

Breath – The Affirmation of Life

If the breathing is all unsettled, life is not your own.

—Qui

The importance of breath in healing

Life begins with a breath, usually accompanied by a sound, as the baby emerges from the womb. We don't need anyone to teach us how to breathe and we carry on doing it all our life, breathing approximately 16 times a minute, 1,080 times an hour, and 21,600 times in a day. We may be able to survive for days without food or water, but not for a moment without breathing. Each of the seventy-five trillion cells in our body absorbs the oxygen we breathe from the atmosphere, and by the process of metabolism, produces the carbon dioxide that we breathe out.

Breathing spans the whole spectrum of healing techniques. In fact it extends beyond the boundaries of healing into the spiritual discipline. This is the miracle of breath: it not only improves physical functions, but also acts as a pathway inward. It is a bridge between the body and the mind, and the mind and the spirit. The Romans used the word *spiritus* for breath. The word means 'spirit', and is part of re*spir*ation in*spir*ation and ex*pir*ation! Breathing influences every cell of the body. It affects our sleep, memory, concentration and our energy levels. Every aspect of our personality depends on our breath.

The wisdom of breathing is omnipresent in various yoga techniques: the physical movements and postures that constitute *Hatha* Yoga; the devotional chanting that is the expression of *Bhakti* Yoga; or the awareness of breath and meditation that is so vital in *Dhyana* Yoga. Our breath is pivotal to our physical, mental, emotional and spiritual well-being. It is the point where all paradigms converge and meet. No healing system can ignore the importance of breathing.

Most of us take our breath for granted, we breathe merely to survive. We are not really aware of our breathing, which is often fast and shallow for various reasons:

• Modern technology and automation have reduced the need for physical activity, and as a result we have less need for deep breathing.

• We give in to emotional outbursts all too soon: we get easily excited, we are quick to anger, and we often suffer from anxiety pangs. Our breathing follows this pattern. More often than not we perform sedentary jobs in a closed environment and our body instinctively inhales less air.

• The body inhales less air to protect itself instinctively from pollution caused by the increased emission particles in the air.

How Do We actually Breathe?

Shallow, rapid, erratic and restricted – these four words aptly describe our normal breathing of which we remain unaware. We neither take in sufficient oxygen nor do we eliminate sufficient carbon dioxide. As a result, our bodies are starved of oxygen, and the toxic build-up leads to generalized physical tension, reduced vitality, emotional instability, confused thought processes, depleted energy, premature aging, poorly functioning immune system, sleep disorders, stomach upsets, muscle cramps, anxiety, dizziness, chest pains, and palpitations.

Why these Faulty Patterns?

These restrictive patterns have gradually developed during our lifetime as the cumulative effect of our experiences. As babies we know how to breathe. Newborn babies breathe with their abdomen, their lower belly rising and falling with each breath. As children grow, they learn to 'hold themselves in' as protection from hurtful comments, emotional knocks, and confusing messages. With advancing age, chronic stress makes the muscles go into a state of tension, preventing the respiratory muscles from functioning fully. Sustained tension in the back muscles and the shoulders due to wrong posture and stress too, can compromise our breathing.

As a consequence, our breathing becomes shallower, proceeding from what is called 'abdominal breathing' to 'chest breathing' and then to 'shoulder breathing'. Older people or those who are seriously ill, breathe shallowly and rapidly, their shoulders rising and falling with every breath. The shallowest breathing is 'throat breathing'. When breathing becomes shallower than this, a person dies.

Conscious Breathing

Just as a correct diet enhances the nutritional essence of the body, correct breathing enhances the supply of vital energy. Left unattended, breathing occurs as spontaneously and naturally as a heartbeat. Unlike the beating of the heart and other involuntary physiological functions of the body, breathing straddles the border of involuntary and voluntary control. We can use our conscious will to alter our breathing, to slow it down, to become deeper. This is called 'conscious breathing'.

Can we, using our free will, command our digestive system to digest food faster, or request the kidneys to filter out the urine slower so that we can enjoy undisturbed sleep? We cannot! Breathing, on the other hand, can be instantaneously controlled or manipulated using our conscious will. Isn't this dimension of physiology a proof that we can improve our breathing and the quality of our life?

When controlled by the mind, breathing becomes as deliberate as walking, and can be made a tool to regulate all other vital functions like blood pressure, digestion, metabolism, pulse rate, hormone secretion, and so on. Our breathing can regulate and control not just the bodily functions, but also the mind. Because of its pivotal role between the body and the mind, breathing is a very important healing tool for health and longevity.

Breathing Our Way to Health

Breath-work may be the simplest and most effective method of healing because breathing is something that everyone does. It is not a question of whether we do it, but how we do it. Breathing is really the most accessible source of creating and sustaining our vital energy.

Becoming aware of our breath is half the job. Changes come about as we develop our awareness by paying closer attention to our breath, and by improving the elasticity and efficiency of our breathing muscles through proper exercises.

The factors that can change our relationship with life through our breath are the pace of breathing, the rhythm we follow, the number of times we breathe, how much breath we allow into our body, the posture of our body when we breathe, the vibrations we produce, the awareness with which we breathe, and our sensitivity to experiencing the effects of breath on the body and the mind. By synchronizing all these aspects while breathing, we will change our relationship with our body and mind.

Our life will change as we begin to breathe differently. Breathing which is naturally light and deep is healthy. Merely watching and focusing on our respiration, and following it along its natural rhythm will cause our breathing to deepen automatically. Once we turn our direction towards this freedom – freedom of the breath, freedom from tension, freedom from holding on to the past—we are on a new road. When we change our breathing, we change everything. Conscious breathing offers the most direct route to better health, confidence and vitality.

9

The Mechanics of Breathing

Breathing corresponds to taking charge of one's life.

—Luce Irigaray

Love more – that is breathing out – and your body will gather energy from the whole cosmos. You create the vacuum and the energy comes.

—Osho

How the breath works in our body.

Our body needs energy on a grand scale. Food is a vital source of energy, but to get this energy in a functional form, oxygen is required. Without oxygen, energy cannot be extracted even from the best of foods. In the presence of oxygen, the nutrients in the food are burnt or broken down in our cells to liberate functional energy, while the carbon dioxide produced gets discarded subsequently.

Food + Oxygen --------→   Carbon dioxide + water + energy

The energy obtained is used to drive each and every function of the body. These functions are collectively called the metabolic functions. Thus, all the activities of the body are performed with the help of the breath, which provides life energy – the force that creates movement, pulsation and the vibration of life. One can live for two months without food, and two weeks without water, but only a few minutes without air. We get this oxygen through our breath by the process of respiration.

Breathing or respiration takes place in a cyclic manner in four steps: inhalation, pause, exhalation, pause. We inhale to absorb the oxygen that is needed to convert food into energy to carry on the various activities of life. When we exhale, we not only discard the carbon dioxide and the impurities, but also create space for new air, new life and new energy. This entire process of exchanging oxygen and carbon dioxide is controlled by nerves, which carry signals from the respiratory control areas of the brain.

Do We Breathe only for Oxygen?

Oxygen is very critical for our well-being, and any effort to increase its supply to our body and brain will pay rich dividends. Oxygen purifies the blood stream, burns up the waste products (toxins), and also recharges the battery of the body. In fact, most of our energy requirements come not from the food we consume but from the air we breathe. People who are regular with their breathing exercises, that is pranayama, often remark that they eat less yet feel very energetic.

This indicates that our breath has something more to offer than just oxygen. The life force that is brought into our being through the breath adds to our vitality and health This life force is not just oxygen, but something subtler – the vital energy, prana, which sustains creation. We have read about the fascinating prana in Chapter 4. Let us now understand the process of breathing and how **nature has devised a wonderful system for the smooth exchange of gases, starting from the nose all the way to the air sacs in the lungs. To aid this continuous act of breathing there are specially designed muscles that coordinate the expansion and contraction of the chest cavity.**

Muscles of respiration

The primary muscles that help us breathe freely are the intercostal muscles, the diaphragm and the abdominal muscles.

Certain neck, shoulder and upper back muscles come into play during extreme activity; these are the secondary breathing muscles. Unfortunately, some of us use these secondary muscles more than the primary ones, and this leads to shoulder and upper back tension.

The intercostal muscles occupy the space between the ribs; they are connected to the spine at the back and the sternum (the breastbone) in the front. These muscles work in a group, lifting the ribs up and out during inhalation, and letting them subside inward and downward during passive exhalation. Healthy action of the intercostal muscles is important for the health and flexibility of the spine. Inadequate movement of the ribs due to shallow breathing can cause the spine to become rigid and inflexible.

The diaphragm is a large dome-shaped, curtain-like muscle, situated between the chest and the abdomen. The heart and the lungs lie above it, and the abdominal organs like the stomach and the liver lie directly underneath it. The diaphragm is attached to the lower end of the sternum, the six lower pairs of ribs, and through extensions, to the upper lumbar vertebrae that make up the arch in the lower back. When the diaphragm moves freely, there is movement in all the structures to which it is attached, and the breath flows in a rhythmic manner.

During inhalation, the diaphragm descends into the abdominal space, causing a partial vacuum in the chest area, and the lungs expand while drawing in air from the atmosphere. As the diaphragm descends into the abdomen, it displaces the abdominal organs that lie beneath it. Therefore, an efficiently working diaphragm massages the liver, the stomach, the kidneys, the pancreas, the spleen, the gall-bladder, and the intestines. Its movement also massages the heart, which rests on top of the diaphragm, which explains how free, rhythmic and relaxed breathing helps maintain a healthy heart.

The abdominal muscles not only support the abdominal organs and the lower back, but also play an active part during exhalation. If we draw these muscles gently back towards the spine, they give the diaphragm a little push so that it rises up and a large volume of impure air is expelled. Therefore our abdominal muscles need to be strong and well toned to do their work. Remember, however, that 'strong' does not mean rigid or tense. In fact during a normal inhalation the muscles should be soft and relaxed so that the descent of the diaphragm is not restricted.

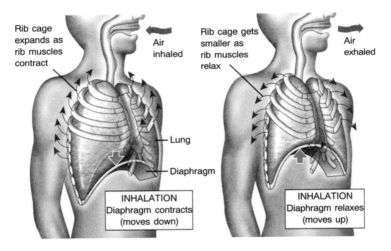

How Is Breathing Controlled?

The nervous system is chiefly responsible for the control and integration of a variety of bodily functions including the lifelong process of breathing. Normal spontaneous breathing takes place without our being really aware of it, without the intervention of consciousness. In those terms, it is an involuntary action going on incessantly as long as one is alive. But breathing can be manipulated, that is, deepened, hastened or slowed down, with the conscious will. When we sing, we do rapid inhalation through the mouth between strings of melody as we continue to exhale. Thus, breathing is the only physiological process in the body that is under the control of both our involuntary and our conscious voluntary nervous system.

A. Involuntary Control of Breathing

There is a very well integrated hierarchy in the way by which our nervous system controls the act of respiration. The controls alter the rate and the depth of breathing in order to meet with the varying oxygen demands of the body. This coordination is done with the help of these 'centres' or loci of specialized cells of the nervous system:

- Medullary respiratory centre, the lower respiratory centre

- Hypothalamus, the upper respiratory centre

The two centres are connected through the Autonomic Nervous System.

Medullary, the Lower Respiratory Centre

This is a respiratory centre in the medulla oblongata, situated in the lower part of the brain stem, where the skull unites with the neck. It maintains the breathing rhythm with the help of nerves passing through the spinal cord, which connect this centre to the muscles of breathing. Changes in the chemical composition of the blood directly affect the lower respiratory centre. Reduced oxygen, excess carbon dioxide, increased pH and acidity of the blood stimulate the centre to increase the rate and the depth of breathing, and vice versa.

As an experiment, hold your breath for five seconds and observe the subsequent breaths – they will be deeper and faster. A deficiency of oxygen and an accumulation of carbon dioxide during the phase of breath-holding immediately stimulate the lower respiratory centre. The centre then sends nerve impulses to the muscles of respiration to deepen and fasten the breaths. So you see how automatically and quickly the system works!

You will also have noticed that, after jogging or any aerobic exercise, the breathing becomes faster and deeper in order to take in more oxygen and remove the extra carbon dioxide that is produced as a result of increased metabolism in the exercising muscles.

Hypothalamus, the Upper Respiratory Centre

The hypothalamus is a small organ located deep between the two sides or hemispheres of the brain. This mini-organ has rich nervous connections with various neuro-endocrine centres in the brain. The hypothalamus works through the autonomic nervous system with its two limbs – the Sympathetic and the Parasympathetic Nervous Systems (see Chapter 2) – to influence other centres, including the lower respiratory centre.

B. Voluntary or Conscious Control

The cortical control, the highest level of nerve control on breathing, comes from the frontal cortex of the brain. The frontal cortex is located just behind the forehead and represents advancement in functions like higher emotions, perception, etc. As this specialized part of the brain has rich nerve connections with various parts of the brain including the breathing centres, our breathing can be easily altered voluntarily or brought under conscious control. In other words, it can bring what is normally instinctive into awareness, or conscious control.

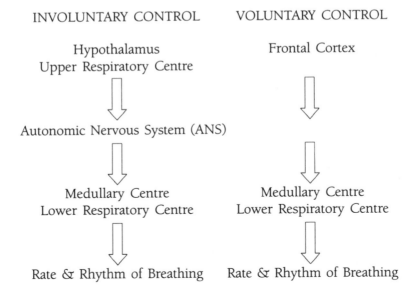

INVOLUNTARY CONTROL   VOLUNTARY CONTROL

Hypothalamus   Frontal Cortex
Upper Respiratory Centre

Autonomic Nervous System (ANS)

Medullary Centre   Medullary Centre
Lower Respiratory Centre   Lower Respiratory Centre

Rate & Rhythm of Breathing   Rate & Rhythm of Breathing

Rhythms in Respiration

Why is the flow of air in the two nostrils unequal at any given time?

Try this simple experiment. Breathe through one nostril at a time instead of both as one unit. Do this by blocking one nostril with your finger and observe the flow in the other for a few breaths. Repeat with the other nostril. You will notice that one nostril is generally more open than the other. Sometimes one side is clear and at other times, for no apparent reason, it seems blocked. You will observe that this is so even though you are not suffering from any allergy or cold.

This is a normal phenomenon occurring in a cyclic manner. There is a natural cyclic change in the congestion of the lining of the nostrils – sometimes the left and sometimes the right. This uni-nostril congestion offers resistance to the movement of air through one particular nostril at a given time. This resistance changes rhythmically from one nostril to another every one and a half to two hours.

Most of us may not be really aware of this rhythm, which is called the nasal cycle. *Swara* Yoga, the science of breath, teaches us about this phenomenon and its effect on our mental state and health. The basic concepts of Swara Yoga, along with the scientific corelates, are explained in Chapter 16.

Our respiration is also under the influence of a rhythmic variation during each twenty-four-hour period of the day and night cycle. This rhythmic change in the pattern of breathing is linked to the Basic Rest Activity Cycle where one alternates between the wakeful and the sleeping states. In the sleeping state the breathing is slow and deep, while in the wakeful state, the breathing is more rapid and shallow.

However, even when we are in the wakeful state our breathing varies depending upon our level of activity and the state of mind. We shall read more about this in the next chapter.

10

Stress Affects Breathing

Our very way of life breeds unhappiness. We have an active and turbulent culture in which there is little peace or contentment.

—David Frawley

How our state of mind affects our breathing.

Every breath we take makes a difference to our body. Be it 'under-breathing' or 'over-breathing', abnormal breathing can have far-reaching effects on our well-being. If we do not breathe correctly, we can suffer long-term chemical, physiological and mental consequences.

Most of the time our breaths run in automatic mode, keeping our nervous, respiratory, cardiac, and muscular systems in functioning order. Normal breathing really requires no effort or thought. We maintain a balance of oxygen and carbon dioxide within the bloodstream, without having to calculate the need for the next breath.

Most of us don't realize how our mental state reflects on our breath. Think about past occasions when you felt scared. Maybe a car pulled suddenly out of a lane, or you saw a small child darting into the traffic, or there was a fire in the house! At these times your heart pounded and your skin turned pale. Your breathing was held back in shock only to be followed by rapid shallow breathing. Should you stay there or should you run? What actually happened was that your autonomic nervous system sensed the alarm and prepared the mind and body for the fight-or-flight response – a mechanism to cope with acute stress.

Stress not only alters our emotional and mental states, but also our breathing. When we are agitated our breathing pattern becomes erratic: we take in the breath, hold it and then let go quickly. The same is the case when we are full of tension. Our breathing becomes irregular and shallow. When we are emotionally agitated, it is difficult to use our best judgement, and we can cause accidents.

Thoughts produce stress, too. For thoughts to move they must have energy. At times the mind is 'racing' while at other times we are 'too tired to think'. As adults, we have learnt to control our speech and breathing. We handle our daily tensions by somehow holding our breath and controlling our thoughts. But thoughts rarely stay controlled, and they can be chaotic. They cause stress in our breathing and spill out in the form of physical illness. Our emotions have a direct effect on our breathing because our emotions and our breathing are closely connected. Think about it: when we are relaxed, calm and satisfied, our breathing is smooth and effortless. Our anxieties produce shallow and erratic breathing, and when we are frightened, breathing is constricted and tight.

The Mechanism: how Stress Affects Breathing

Our Autonomic Nervous System (ANS) serves as a neural matrix, a junction point for coupling our state of mind with the body, where psychology meets physiology, significantly affecting the functions of the body.

The ANS is designed to maintain a balance between various functions of the body, and to keep us mentally balanced between extreme anxiety and functional calm. It functions through its two wings – the Sympathetic Nervous System (SNS) and the Parasympathetic System (PNS).

The SNS prepares us for emergencies and acute physical and mental stressors by triggering the fight-or-flight response, which manifests itself by altering the pulse, blood pressure, body temperature, respiration and brain waves. So we become 'symptomatic' of stress, and exhibit shallow, rapid breathing. This is an autonomic response, but also the first step towards distress and ill health. The PNS works to balance the response to stress and to 'ease and release' the effects.

Emotional upsurges and excitatory impulses instantaneously pass down through the hypothalamus-SNS link to increase the rate of breathing. Inhalation primarily relates to the SNS, which encourages us to take action and cope with the various stressors. Exhalation relating to the PNS assists us in letting go and restoring our equilibrium. So, with a balance of inhalation and exhalation, we are able to stay centred and focused, reacting appropriately to situations.

But are we actually breathing that way? No, not at all! In reality, due to our fast- paced life, we are more or less in a state of near-constant stress, with one or the other stressor knocking on our psychological framework. Unknowingly, we fail to give an opportunity to our PNS to take over, so that the stressors and their effects might get nullified. Our Sympathetic Nervous System is overtaxed, leading to a host of diseases. Our breathing too, is not as it should be.

Let us first become aware of how we breathe normally.

Shallow Breathing

Quick and shallow breathing is the trademark of stress. It takes place primarily in the upper part of the chest and the lungs. Also known as high breathing, it is restricted to the collarbone and the shoulders, and reaches at most to mid-chest level. In this type of breathing, the lower parts of the lungs are practically unventilated. There is no exchange of air, and the stale air accumulates in the lungs. This is the least desirable form of breathing as it prevents us from taking in sufficient oxygen and eliminating sufficient carbon dioxide.

As a result, a toxic build-up occurs in the body, leading to reduced vitality, premature aging, and a poor immune system. This form of breathing is so common that it is accepted as the norm. However, it often leads to physical tension, digestive disorders, lethargy, emotional instability, a confused thought process, and concomitant stress. Lack of sufficient oxygen is also a major contributing factor in heart disease, cancer and paralytic stroke.

Reverse Breathing

This is a habit born out of being constantly anxious and fearful. As we experience fear, our normal sympathetic response is to inhale and hold our breath. The belly gets sucked in at the same time, as if winded. This is exactly the opposite of what we would be doing if breathing normally. We then hold our breath until the danger passes. After that, quickly and with an outward sigh, we release both the belly and the breath.

Reverse breathing is actually contrary to the natural flow of our body. It habituates us to inhaling improperly by pulling the abdomen in and reducing the lung volume. Exhalations, too, are incomplete as the outward paradoxical movement of the belly prevents proper emptying of the lungs.

Curtailed Exhalations

Exhalation is a very important part of the breathing process because that is when we really discard the impurities through the lungs in the form of carbon dioxide. What deep breathing does, exhalation can do even better. Exhalation tries to slow the quick and shallow breathing. It is important, therefore, to pay attention to the way we exhale. Taking in a few quick deep breaths is not a quick fix for any ailment. What we really need to do is to breathe out completely. A few full exhalations will help to release tensions, calm us physically and emotionally, and also restore our free rhythmic breathing.

Slimmer's Breath

Some people habitually hold in their abdominal muscles to

appear slimmer. This tension obstructs the breathing process, making it shallow and restricted. Not only do the cells get deprived of oxygen, but the abdominal organs too, are deprived of a vital health-giving massage. When a person is in a hurry to inhale, the exhalation gets curtailed. Failure to use the diaphragm makes him use the secondary breathing muscles of the neck and the shoulders, creating tension and stress. Many of us have grown up breathing incorrectly this way, and experience tiredness for no apparent reason.

Instead of pulling in tightly all the abdominal muscles, we would do better with a mild toning of the muscle that is at a transverse below the navel, called the Transverse Abdominis (TA). In fact, this muscle is close to our six- or eight-pack 'abs', and a baseline tone in the TA supports the abdominal organs optimally without obstructing the breathing.

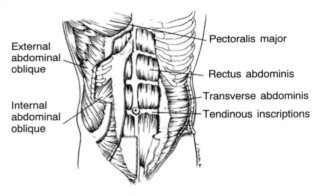

Muscles of the Trunk

Poor Breathing and Fatigue

Are you constantly tired? Do you feel drained out by midday? Do you take vitamin supplements? Subject yourself to a battery of tests, only to get normal results that do not explain the fatigue? Is it all just in your mind? The answer is simple, if not so obvious. Poor quality of breathing is the underlying cause of all your symptoms. This includes muscle cramps, chest pains, premenstrual tensions and headaches.

When we are chronically in a state of stress, we tax our SNS. As a result we are always operating on the threshold. Eventually, the body refuses to take the load and a constant background fatigue sets in.

As stress becomes more a part of our lives than not, the tone of the SNS takes the upper hand over that of the PNS. As our Sympathetic Nervous System is chronically stimulated, this leads to 'more-than-what-it-should-be' levels of:

- Heart rate
- Blood pressure
- Muscular tension
- Blood sugar levels

| Inhalation | >>>> | Exhalation |
| SNS | >>>> | PNS |

This affects us on a deeper physical and emotional level. When we cannot cope further, the body breaks down and we are struck down with all kinds of illnesses. More than 70 per cent of our modern-day diseases are psychosomatic illnesses originating in the mind. Thus our mind, emotions, thought processes, reactions and actions are at the root of disease genesis.

Creating Well-Being through the Breath

Nature has provided a very powerful tool to combat the harmful effects of stress – our PNS. All we need to do is understand and implement techniques to activate its functioning. What are these techniques? Sleep, relaxation, pranayama, meditation, music, soft emotions, love, compassion, forgiveness, and acceptance, are some of the ways to energize the functions of the Parasympathetic Nervous System.

Conscious breathing holds a very special place here. Our breath is the first to get affected by stress. The good news is that respiration is the only response to stress that can be altered and controlled using our conscious will, even though it is monitored by the Autonomic Nervous System. Our breathing can be manipulated easily, and at will, not only to neutralize the effects of stress on the body but also to add more energy or prana to the system.

Correct breathing can help us a great deal in maintaining good health. With our breathing we can influence our nervous system, transform our mental, emotional and even our physical health, and maintain well-being. How we breathe, and how much we give ourselves a chance to breathe 'consciously' every day, can strongly influence our health. Thus, we can improve our stress responses by honing our skills – regulating our breath and emotions, and governing the mind.

We can actually alter our emotional state by influencing our breath. It is a remarkable discovery indeed! So remarkable in fact that I would like to reiterate it. **We can alter our emotional state by influencing our breathing.**

Conscious Breathing – Magnetize the Mind

Taking a deep breath is like combing the energy in and around us. It is like getting up in the morning with dishevelled hair, but, as we brush and smooth the hair down, we give it direction and in turn, feel fresh and energized. Breathing does more or less the same thing to our state of mind. With deep inhalations and exhalations we align or 'comb' the energy around us. This enables us to remain calmer and more focused. The energy which is focused becomes a magnet, attracting like polarities towards us.

Instead of having a confused mind with disarrayed molecules we now have a focused, magnet-like mind with the north and south poles perfectly matched. A magnet energizes a piece of plain metal into alignment with itself, causing a second magnet to emerge. Similarly, when we practise correct breathing, our energies align, resulting in the mind, body and wisdom focusing and acting as one. This is centred energy in action.

How To Breathe when under Stress

Regulating the breath can help us in many situations. When we feel overburdened, we ease ourselves with a few sighs (full exhalations through the mouth). Sighing helps to break the cycle of tension. A minute or two of breathers – long, full and smooth exhalations – can work wonders.

At such times we must take a moment to adjust the pattern: breathe in and out without straining, let the breathing be free, slow, deep and rhythmic. Gradually, our agitated thoughts will calm down, and if we stay with this pattern long enough, we will be amazed at how effectively it works. The best way to defuse anger quickly or decrease frustration is to simply stop thinking and take a deep breath.

Breathing techniques influence the sympathetic-parasympathetic balance. By breathing slowly and deeply, we initiate a Parasympathetic Nervous System reaction, whereby the heart slows down, the blood pressure lowers, and the loop slows down the mental chaos. And then we wonder what we were so excited about!

When we breathe slowly – especially while exhaling – it gives our thoughts space to spread out. As we allow space between the breaths, a similar space is created between thoughts, resulting in clarity and wisdom. We have a better understanding of the life situation, and then comes the insight for taking the right steps for restoring the balance. Deep breathing will quieten the emotions and enable us to access our circumstances in a better way.

For example, a film is made up of multiple frames which are run at a particular speed in order to present us with a continuous scenario. If any changes have to be made, the film has to be run at a slow speed, so that each frame can be seen separately. The frame with the error is identified and corrected. Thus, awareness of breathing can bring vitality and enjoyment to each moment of our life. By exhaling slowly we know whether any strain or stress has crept into our body or mind. Our breathing becomes a good barometer for relaxation or stress.

It is important to note that at first it may be difficult to obtain perfect results. Persistence, however, pays and success will be ours eventually.

Pranayama, the breathing practices of yoga involving slow diaphragmatic breathing, has been found to shift overall basal autonomic balance to the parasympathetic direction. This reduces the adverse psycho-physiological and psychological effects of chronic stress, and reactivity in stressful situations. The stress-reducing benefits of slow, deep, diaphragmatic breathing in patients with heart disease, hypertension and asthma, have made these breathing practices a valuable component of many integrated treatment programmes.

The Approach

Most people do not breathe the right way. So our first task, before starting any special breathing exercises, is to learn how to breathe correctly. Any exaggeration or performance of pranayama when the body has not been prepared can cause breathing difficulties and uncomfortable symptoms and signs, such as nervousness, shortness of breath, unstable blood pressure and palpitations.

Remember, any tension or discomfort during pranayama is a sign that the body is not yet prepared, and that we have to improve its performance through basic breathing exercises. We have to train and adapt our breathing organs and centres, and all the other breathing functions, to these new patterns of breathing in a smooth, gradual, natural and unforced way.

We are now all set to begin this journey towards health – a journey that starts with breath awareness, and through the practice of pranayama (yogic breathing exercises), leads us towards health of the body and the mind. We will proceed in the following sequence:

- Normal breathing
- Conscious breathing
- Pranayama for the body
- Pranayama for creating an optimum state of mind
- Techniques of tapping the healing powers of the mind

11

Conscious Deep-Breathing

The 'you' that goes in one side of the breathing experience is not the same 'you' that comes out the other side.

—Bhante Henepola

As all the small rivulets flow into the sea, so should the attention point to the breath within.

—Swami Nityananda

How correct breathing can benefit us immensely.

In our normal breathing we take in about 500 ml of air. As the average lung capacity is 4000-5000 ml, the amount of air exchanged in normal breathing is hardly 10 per cent, which is surprisingly small for the volume of our lungs. The oxygen-rich air we breathe in reaches only the mid-lungs; it does not go to the upper and the lower lobes of the lungs. We can, therefore, breathe out only this 500 ml of air. The lower and the upper lobes are filled with oxygen-deprived air that they have stored and are unable to breathe out. This could be one of the reasons why tuberculosis is prevalent in the upper lobes of the lungs, and pneumonia in the lower lobes.

As babies, we belly-breathe, developing our lower lungs first. There is a natural, gentle, rhythmic, in-and-out motion as the belly expands and contracts. This enables the lower part of the lungs to receive oxygen. The middle part of the chest and the lungs develop next, followed by the upper lungs or the apex as the baby indulges in more activity and movement. As adults, we tend to keep the belly still when we breathe. The stressors of life take so much of our awareness that we breathe rapidly and shallowly, trying to match the pace of life.

Breathing more deeply for just a few breaths can pep us up when we are fatigued by the frantic pace of the day. Then with a little practice, it can become a regular feature of the day.

Exhalations Are Important to Good Health

As adults, our hurry-and-worry type of living reflects in our shallow and rapid breathing and curtailed exhalations. We have not only forgotten how to breathe correctly, but the ratio between our inhalations and exhalations too, is quite erratic. When we breathe optimally and in a relaxed way, there is a natural ratio of 1:2 in the length of inhalation and exhalation. This means that the exhalation is twice as long as the inhalation: if we inhale for four seconds the exhalation should normally last about eight seconds, without our feeling any discomfort.

A full and unrestricted exhalation is more vital than only a deep inhalation. It is during this exhalation that the relaxation response gets triggered. With a long and slow exhalation, the PNS gets activated and toned. This initiates the relaxation response, restoring inner balance. The smooth, quiet, relaxed and flowing breathing that is the outcome of awareness slows the heartbeat and lowers the blood pressure. It also produces a sense of stability and a positive feeling of security. Breathing this new, deeper way actually encourages the heart to rest because the long exhalations slow down the heart rate, giving the heart more time to relax.

A good exhalation results naturally in a subsequent fuller and unforced inhalation. With regular practice the breath becomes free, more steady and deep, without any conscious effort on our part. As the breath flows, the energy too, flows, calming the SNS. It reduces stress, and enhances our physical, emotional and mental health.

This is achieved through regular daily practice, ideally from the time of our first introduction to breathing exercises. However, we should by no means force ourselves to achieve the mentioned 1:2 ratio in order to progress more rapidly because, sooner or later, the body will react negatively to this forced way of breathing. We have to come to it gradually, because only then will the body adapt naturally, avoiding any later problems.

How to proceed

- Correct the posture
- Identify reverse breathing
- Correct reverse breathing
- Practise three-part breathing

Posture

While practising any breathing exercise, it is important that the spine be kept straight, so as not to impede the free flow of air. This can be accomplished by sitting in any of the following positions (refer Chapter 14 for some more practical details):

1. **Cross-legged position on the mat**: to sit comfortably on a mat or the floor for a long time, sit cross-legged on a pillow to elevate your tail bone. Keep the spine straight, head erect, mouth closed, and hands relaxed on the knees or in the lap, palm on palm.

2. **Sitting on a firm chair with a ninety-degree angle between the seat and the back**: if sitting on the floor makes you feel uncomfortable and stiff, particularly in the hip region, the lower back or the knees, sit on a chair, instead. It is better to enjoy the subtle effects of breathing on the mind and the body, rather than get distracted by physical discomfort.

3. **Lying down flat on the back with legs folded or straight, whichever is comfortable**: a thin pillow to keep the neck in line with the spine promotes deep comfortable breathing.

Cross legged sitting   Correct sitting on chair
                                              with cushion

Identifying Reverse Breathing

If the stomach caves in instead of bulging out during deep
inhalation, and vice versa, we are doing what is known as
reverse breathing which is very common. A few deep breaths
done with awareness and with the palms placed on the belly will
instantaneously identify reverse breathing.

Correcting Reverse Breathing

• Place both hands on the belly region.

• **Begin with exhalation**, as the first step is to enable the belly
to reunite in the act of breathing. As you breathe **out** ... **press**
the belly **in** ... and release with inhalation. In order to
experience the flow of the breath, imagine that there is some
dust in the nose and you are trying to blow it out. Naturally the
breath would go **out** and the belly would go **in**.

• During inhalation, relax the abdomen without allowing it to
bulge out.

Practising this several times can really help correct the pattern.
Initially one may have to concentrate in order to correct a now-
automatic response. After a few sessions you will feel the

difference, and the body, which was fashioned to breathe paradoxically, will fully co-operate.

When we consciously push the belly inside, we activate the diaphragm, allowing the air from the lower lungs to leave the body. The inhalation that follows will be deeper than when the diaphragm does not move, pushing the diaphragm down and allowing a larger quantity of air to flow into the lungs.

As you continue this exercise, the exhalation should gradually increase until it becomes twice as long as the inhalation. Our primary focus is on the exhalation and letting go. The inhalation then comes back in naturally. If we breathe with an attitude of gratitude, a heart full of joy, and a smile on our lips, the breathing becomes lighter! We achieve freedom of the breath, and freedom from tension.

Self-correction in a Lying-down Position

We breathe naturally and deeply while lying down or sleeping. Nature is so benign that merely by lying down and breathing we can spontaneously correct our faulty pattern of breathing. So lie down, close your eyes, relax your body and observe your breathing. Initially one can place a book on the stomach, and observe it moving up and down with the stomach as one breathes.

Deep Conscious Breathing

Deep breathing is closely related to the movement of the diaphragm, the dome-shaped muscular structure that separates the chest from the abdomen. When we breathe deeply, our diaphragm moves downward as we inhale, and upward as we exhale. The more the diaphragm moves, the more our lungs can expand, which means that more oxygen can be taken in and more carbon dioxide released with each breath.

The *complete breath* technique, also called three-part breathing, slowly fills and empties the entire lung capacity. You can accomplish a smooth maximum inhalation by first expanding the abdomen and the lower ribcage, then expanding the middle ribcage, and finally expanding the upper ribcage. The abdomen withdraws naturally as the chest is fully expanded. A slow maximum exhalation follows in the reverse order – lowering the upper chest, then the middle chest, and finally pulling in the abdomen.

To understand the direction of the flow of air, let us visualize a balloon that fills from the bottom up. When you release the air it empties from the top first. Similarly, our lungs start filling from the lower part, proceeding upwards as we inhale. The emptying of the lungs begins from the upper part of the chest towards the lower part of the lungs. To understand this coordination, place the right hand on the stomach and the left hand on the chest. This can be done in either a sitting or a standing position. Focus the mind on the breath and the release of tension during breathing. Ensure that breaths are slow, continuous, smooth and flowing, without any interruption. There should be no effort or strain. As the awareness increases, we can feel the functions of the diaphragm.

1. Begin by exhaling completely through the nose. When the exhalation is complete, the stomach, and the right hand placed on it, will move in. At the end of the exhalation the stomach should contract.

2. Begin the inhalation by expanding the stomach, with the right hand still on it. Allow the lower lungs to fill. Continue to inhale allowing the lower ribcage to expand. The upper chest will also fill up slowly.

3. While exhaling, release the air from the upper chest, then the lower chest and finally, the abdomen section, one smoothly flowing into the other. Inhale, continuing to expand the abdomen, the lower chest, the middle chest and the upper chest, so that the collarbones rise slightly. Continue breathing slowly and deeply for a few minutes, ending with an exhalation.

It is important to note that the chest muscles and the lungs may not be used for such expansion, so one must be careful about any untoward strain or dizziness. If you feel tired or short of breath, it is advisable to return to normal breathing for a while before resuming. Stress or strain actually depletes the life force, wiping out many of the good effects of correct breathing.

Benefits of Slow and Deep Breathing

In deep breathing, the rhythmic movements of the diaphragm help to detoxify our inner organs, promote blood flow, improve peristalsis, and pump more fluid through our lymphatic system.

Blood

An improved quality of blood is a direct result of increased oxygenation of the lungs. All the cells benefit from the oxygen and, as a result, all the toxins are flushed out of the body.

Lungs

The lungs become stronger and more elastic. Deep breathing actually saves the breath by slowing down and deepening the respiratory pattern. This brings about efficiency in the gas exchange and has an economizing effect.

Heart

Yogic breathing reduces the workload on the heart in two ways:

• As the efficiency of the lungs increases, the oxygen-carrying capacity of the blood increases, and the heart does not have to work so hard to deliver oxygen to the tissues.

• Owing to greater pressure differential in the lungs due to deep breathing, there is an increase in circulation, thus giving the heart a little rest. The heart operates better and lives longer, keeping blood pressure and other heart diseases under control.

Abdominal Organs

The increased movement of the diaphragm during deep breathing massages the organs, namely the stomach, the liver, the pancreas, the bowels and the heart. This results in a better flow of blood to the organs, and leads to better absorption of food, better digestion, better bowel movement, detoxification through the liver, and so on.

Nervous System

Improvement in the health and tone of the nervous system is due only to better oxygenation. This improves the health of the whole body as the nervous system communicates with all the parts of the body.

Endocrine System

All the endocrine, that is, the hormone-secreting, glands get rejuvenated, especially the pituitary and the pineal glands in the brain. The brain requires three times more oxygen than the rest of the body. By nurturing these master endocrine glands in the brain, deep breathing has far-reaching effects on our well-being.

Weight Control

Oxygen burns up excess fat more efficiently, and in an underweight person, this oxygen feeds the starving tissues and glands. In other words, the inhaled oxygen offers the ideal weight for the individual.

Relaxation

Slow, deep and rhythmic breathing causes a reflex stimulation of the PNS, which causes a reduction in the heart rate and relaxation of the muscles. This also relaxes the mind as the mind and the body are interdependent. Better oxygenation of the brain helps reduce excessive anxiety levels. We will begin to like ourselves as we feel the calming and pleasing sensation that conscious deep breathing brings. A sense of deep undisturbed peace and well-being will be felt within.

SECTION IV
PRANAYAMA

If you can do something with the breath,
you will suddenly turn to the present.

If you can do something with the breath,
you will attain to the source of life.

If you can do something with the breath,
you can transcend time and space.

If you can do something with the breath,
you will be in the world and also beyond it.

—Anonymous

12

The Power of Pranayama

Yogic breathing is based on rhythm, and rhythm is life.

—James Hewitt

Only when we are willing to give away every last particle of breath, which is our life force, can we truly receive.

—Gurmukh

Managing the breath is an art that we can all learn.

The mind and the body are connected with each other by a vibrant system of inner energy that is sustained by the flow of the breath. Thus, life, energy and breath are inseparable and deeply linked with each other. Practices that make us conscious of this system constitute the science and art of Pranayama.

Pranayama is the yogic science of balancing and regulating vital energy or prana through the skilful manipulation of breath. Rishi Patanjali has defined pranayama as 'the regulation of the incoming and outgoing flow of breath'.

This science has been preserved for us through many generations, both in practice and in handwritten books. Pranayama is the crux, the most valuable component of yoga, because its techniques have been tested by time and have been practised successfully for centuries.

Pranayama, as commonly conceived, involves much more than

mere breathing exercises. It also denotes cosmic power, or the power of the entire universe, which manifests itself in us as a conscious living being, through the phenomenon of breathing.

The universal law of sustenance is the law of rhythm. Rhythm pervades the universe: from the movement of the planets around the sun to the movement of atoms in the cells, there is rhythm. Our bodies too, are subject to natural rhythms called biorhythms, such as the sleep-wake cycle, the menstrual cycle in females, and the hormones and associated functions.

Breathing too, is the rhythm of life. Poor breathing disturbs the rhythm of bodily functions. Pranayamic breathing exercises are more than deep-breathing practices. Pranayama allows the body to re-establish its own natural rhythm and get attuned to the cosmic rhythm, thereby promoting holistic health.

The word pranayama is made up of two words – *prana* and *ayama*. They are understood as 'breath' and 'control', or control over the movement of breath. Ayama means the action or the voluntary effort to control, direct and regulate this prana. When the self-energizing force embraces the body and the mind with expansion and control through voluntary regulation of the breath, it is pranayama.

It is mentioned in the yogic texts: 'He who practises pranayama will have good digestive power, cheerfulness, a lean figure, strength, stamina, courage, enthusiasm, a good standard of health, vigour and vitality, and a good concentration of mind.'

When we do pranayama, prana, the vital life force, flows abundantly into us through our breaths. It gets transformed into various powers in the body to carry out the different internal and external functions.

Breathing is a very important part of the body's elimination processes, and pranayama too, helps us rid ourselves of what we no longer need. Through the breath we discard the toxic gas, carbon dioxide, the by-product of metabolism in the body. Regular practice of pranayama eliminates physical and mental toxins.

Pranayama for the Mind

Without the help of prana the mind cannot operate because the vibrations of prana produce thoughts in the mind. Breath is the external manifestation of prana—breath is gross and prana is subtle. So, mind, prana and breath are interrelated.

Pranayama is the tool that links the body and the mind through the breath. Through pranayama, that is, by exercising control over the breath, we can control the subtle prana inside. This control of prana means control of the mind, so, control of breath is control of both prana and the mind.

We can use our breath to free the mind of blocks, thus leading to greater clarity. Little wonder that pranayama is considered to be the highest form of purification and self-discipline for the mind.

The Yoga Sutras of Rishi Patanjali say,

Tatah shriyate prakaashanarnam' (PYS II – 52).

When we practise pranayama, the veil of lethargy and ignorance is gradually drawn away from the mind, and there is an increase in clarity and mind power. Pranayama gives purity, allowing the light of wisdom to shine.

Physiological Effects of Pranayama

Through pranayama techniques the bloodstream, the heart, the lungs, the brain, the tissues and the other organs get enriched with vitalizing energy. This brings about a change in the coordination of physical functions and mental attitudes. Investigations have revealed that the practice of pranayama helps the functioning of the body in many ways:

• **Respiratory system**: Pranayama results in increased elasticity of lungs, enhanced vital capacity and lung functioning, cultured respiratory muscles, better gas exchange, slower respiratory rate, and ease of breathing.

• **Circulatory system**: It facilitates massage to the heart by the movement of the diaphragm, efficient functioning, a slower heart rate and better collateral (natural blood vessels for the heart muscles) formation.

• **Digestive system:** Pranayama enables the diaphragm and the abdominal muscles to massage the stomach, the intestines, the liver, and the pancreas.

• **Central nervous system:** It influences the higher functions of the Central Nervous System (CNS), such as perception, planning, execution of tasks, learning and memory. It improves coherence between the two cerebral hemispheres signifying synchronization of the logical and the intuitive functions. It also increases alertness, along with relaxation as alpha waves dominate the brain's activity, leading to less nervous irritability. This also results in less neuroticism, decreased mental fatigue, and improved awareness.

• **Peripheral nervous system:** Pranayama results in better circulation to the spinal nerves, better nerve impulse transmission, and toning of the Autonomic Nervous System, creating an inner balance or homeostasis.

• **Endocrine system:** It results in richer blood supply to the hormone- secreting glands, leading to balanced glandular activity and hormonal profile; also to decreased activity of the adrenocortical (the endocrine gland which discharges the stress hormones) gland, which can be interpreted as increased ability to resist stress.

• **Anti-oxidant effect:** It significantly lowers the amount of dangerous free radicals, at the same time contributing to a modest increase in the body's intrinsic quantities of health-promoting antioxidants.

Rewards of Pranayama

1. **Stress management:** Pranayama is the best method of managing stress as it progressively trains the mind to learn to listen to itself. The external sounds and the incessant demands of day-to-day living suppress the rational mind. Pranayama trains us to reach the core of stillness despite all the disturbances around us.

Under stress, our Autonomic Nervous System, which has been designed by nature to protect us, tends to overreact and balances precriously on the threshold. At this juncture, pranayama works by strengthening and muscling up our inhibitory response to the stress-handling mechanisms of the body, which produce distress instead of protecting us.

2. **Positive change in attitude:** Kapalabhati clears the mind instantly of all subconscious disturbing elements, and generates a wave of positivity, thus overcoming depression. It is like a cup of instant coffee! During pranayama, the breathing is consciously made slow, deep and rhythmic. This brings about a balanced, tranquil and relaxed state of well-being. Our instincts, desires, and ego come under control and cannot interfere with the mind. This brings about a positive change in behaviour, and can, eventually, transform the total personality.

3. **Breath awareness:** Pranayama is not just about bringing the inhalation and the exhalation into a certain relationship with each other. It is also about using the various techniques and ratios of breathing for developing greater awareness. This helps draw the mind away from the unhealthy chatter of thoughts. During pranayama the attention is on the various aspects of breath, and it is very important to have an alert mind to sense and feel the movement of the breath within.

4. **Inner awareness and sensitivity:** Paying attention to the breath brings our conscious brain, the neo-cortex, into operation. Breathing is thus in our conscious control rather than being an automatic and mechanical activity governed by the ANS.

Inner awareness is not just attention – it is attention with inner sensitivity. During the initial learning phase of pranayama, our attention on the breathing results in fast progress. Soon however, the process becomes mechanical, and a sense of stagnation and lack of interest take over. Awareness builds up when attention is combined with sensitivity. Unfortunately, sensitivity is difficult to find. The practice of various pranayama techniques can help us develop inner sensitivity as well.

6. **Third-person attitude:** Regular practice helps us gain control over our emotions, resulting in inner calm, balance and a third-person attitude (*sakshi bhaava*). What psychologists call our rational mind, Indian philosophy calls the witnessing self, which can analyse without getting emotionally carried away.

7. **Mind power:** This is the main aim of pranayama. When the mind is at a standstill, no thoughts or emotions disturb it. We can control our temperament, desires, mood swings, and instincts with the practice of pranayama.

Hathapradipika says very aptly (HP II: 2):

'Chale vate chalam chittam, nischale nischalam bhavet,
Yogi sthanutvamaprotitato vayum nirodhayet.'

That is, 'As long as breathing continues, the mind remains unstable; when the breath is controlled the activity of the mind is also controlled.'

8. **Preparation for meditation:** With the consistent and committed practice of pranayama, spontaneous pauses start to occur during the phases of breathing. The mind turns absolutely blank – a rare state of stillness and peace for which we all yearn. This happens because the inner chatter of irrational thoughts that keep bombarding our mental frame gets filtered out, and the mind becomes steady, peaceful and more suitable for concentration and the practice of meditation.

Therefore the mind should be applied to the practice of pranayama, making internal awareness an integral and obligatory part. This helps to divert our awareness, from its usual occupation with the body and its surroundings, to the more subtle activities taking place in the mind. We can then reach a state of peace, bliss and health.

A mechanical protocol of inhaling and exhaling bound by ratios is not enough. Prana enters deeply as soon as a positive change occurs in the mind. Changes of mind can be primarily observed in our relationships with the people in our life. Relationships, and how we handle them, are the real test of how to actually understand ourselves.

9. **Handling diseases:** Science has accepted the role of the mind and the psyche in somatic or physical diseases. With the judicious practice of pranayama one can attain a sound healthy state, a steady and peaceful mind, and a lustrous body (HP II 16-18).

10. **Purification:** The practice of pranayama purifies the subtle channels (nadis) through which energy flows. These nadis permit the passage of prana, nerve impulses, and lymph or blood in the spaces between the cells. By cleaning these channels, pranayama helps to eradicate toxins from the body and the mind. Toxins, *mala* in yogic language, give rise to an imbalance in the body and mind by obstructing the normal functioning of the nadis.

A Taoist text from China too, has pointed out the superiority of breathing practices. In the words of Shen Chai-shu, a Ching dynasty adept and physician, 'Breathing and related exercises are a hundred times more effective as medical therapy than any drug. This knowledge is indispensable to man, and every physician should study it thoroughly.'

Even in Russia and Europe, physicians have discovered this ancient remedy. In the words of the French physicians, Dr. Paschier and Walter Michel, 'Every functional or organic disorder leading to conditions of illness is susceptible to the influence, if not always the cure, of controlled breathing.'

Controlled respiration is the most outstanding method known to us for increasing organic resistance. Reduce the organic resistance and you will see germs, which up to that moment had been non-injurious, developing into agents of infection.

There is always a natural immunity attributed to ionic balance in the blood, and proper, controlled breathing confers on that balance of the acid base, a regularity which is re-established with each breath.

By controlling the act of breathing and prana, we can efficiently gain control over the body and the mind. The breath, directed by thought under the control of our will, is a vitalizing and regenerating force that can be utilized for self-development, for healing many diseases, and for gaining control over our character and circumstances. It is within easy reach at every moment of our life. Let us use it judiciously.

Regular practice of Pranayama is like putting money in the bank – it develops a reserve of health, energy and vitality upon which we can draw long after we have finished our practice.

—Richard C. Miller

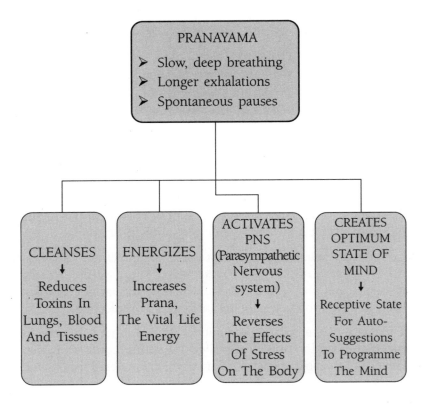

13

The Principles and Language of Pranayama

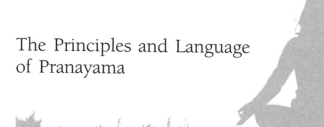

Learning is movement from moment to moment.

—J. Krishnamurti

Pranayama is a process of transforming our individual energy into cosmic energy.

—Kevin Kingsland

It's all so unique and subtle.

History of Pranayama

The earliest reference to pranayama is found in Vedic literature, dating back to before 1500 BC. At that time, pranayama was practised mainly as part of religious ceremonies when the breath was held while reciting mantras in the mind. This was done to control the wavering of the mind and to make the recitation of the mantra more fruitful.

Over time the effects of pranayama on the mind surfaced in clearer terms. The most important milestone in the evolution of pranayama came when Rishi Patanjali (300 BC), through his Yoga Sutras described pranayama as a psycho-physiological practice, and a technique that led to mastery over the mind, *manojaya*. He acknowledged that the manipulation of the breathing activity had a great physiological and psychological effect that could be utilized to improve the health of the mind-body complex.

Pranayama techniques were later harnessed and classified in the Hatha Yogic tradition (1000–1700 AD). The deliberate stopping of breath, *Kumbhaka,* became the most important component of pranayama, so much so that the word Kumbhaka was used as a synonym for pranayama. In this tradition, methods of manipulating the breath using *bandhas,* and *shatakriyas* like *Kapalabhati* and *Bhastrika*, and hand and finger positions for directing prana evolved. Details about the phases of breathing, their speed and ratios, and types and techniques of retention of breath, were added at this time.

At this juncture, one can say that there are two schools of thought as far as pranayama is considered. One has a greater degree of freedom as it lays more importance on the fine and subtle effects on the mind through gentle practices depending on one's capacity, while the other emphasizes the technical aspect of the practice.

Basic Principles and Aims of Doing Pranayama

Pranayama is consciously slowing down and controlling the process of breathing to break the involuntary control that is going on. This happens as we gain control over breathing by overriding the involuntary control (the lower centre) with conscious control, using the higher cortical centre (the neo-cortex). The basic aims of doing pranayama are:

- Slowing down the breathing rate
- Taking complete breaths
- Exhaling more completely and effectively
- Balancing the breaths
- Building awareness
- Effortless retention of breaths

Exhalations Are Important

In pranayama, the emphasis is on proper and prolonged exhalation. It is during exhalation that we throw out toxins from the body in the form of carbon dioxide. If the quality of exhalation is not good, the entire practice of pranayama gets adversely affected.

Benefits of a Good and Deep Exhalation

- More impurities are discarded through the lungs.

- The abdominal muscles and the diaphragm can be used in a more beneficial way. The internal abdominal organs get a good massage.

- Long exhalation triggers the PNS, bringing about a balanced and calm state of mind as PNS helps combat the effects of stress.

- The subsequent inhalation automatically gets deepened and the overall quality of breath improves.

- The mind gets time to relax and recoup from the effects of stress, and this has a positive effect on the state of the physical body.

If we are unable to breathe out slowly and smoothly, without strain, we are not really ready to progress in pranayama. Therefore, beginning any breathing practice with exhalation sets it on the right track.

Language of Pranayama

Pranayama comprises three processes: Rechaka, Pooraka, Kumbhaka.

Rechaka (Exhalation): Rechaka is the phase of breathing out the impure air from the lungs in a smooth and continuous manner. In normal breathing, muscular energy is used for inhaling, while exhaling involves merely relaxing the tensed muscles. In pranayamic breathing, the abdominal muscles are used under constant control to prolong the exhalation over the inhalation, and also to force more air out of our system.

The abdomen that may have bulged out during inhalation now starts contracting and moving inward. This helps evacuate the lungs by raising the diaphragm. The chest, which had expanded, starts contracting, and air flows out through the nostrils. Unless we first breathe out fully, it is impossible to breathe in correctly. After a good exhalation, greater volumes of fresh air automatically enter the lungs.

Pooraka (Inhalation): Pooraka is the process of drawing in air in a smooth and continuous manner. After emptying the lungs, the next step is to fill them up to the maximum possible extent. In deep-breathing practice, the chest expands and the diaphragm gets pushed down. The organs inside the abdominal cavity get pushed down, and the front wall of the abdomen gets pushed out. The process of Pooraka is theoretically slightly different. The lungs fill up and the diaphragm descends, but the muscles of the front wall of the abdomen and those in the perianal region are kept under constant control, and the abdominal wall is prevented from getting pushed out.

However, if we get unduly stressed trying to keep the abdominal wall in place, we miss the subtler effects on the mind. Therefore, it is important to breathe as gently as possible with a constant flow and rhythm. We must learn to be aware of the breath coming in through the nostrils, the flowing air touching the back of the throat and further inside behind the chest bone, the ribs and the chest wall expanding, and the gradual rise in pressure inside the abdominal cavity.

Kumbhaka (Breath Retention): Traditionally, the systematic holding of the breath is called Kumbhaka. The word Kumbhaka means a pitcher or a pot to hold or retain matter and in the context of pranayama, it means 'to hold the breath or the movement of air'.

Types of Kumbhaka

A. Time-based

   1. Antara Kumbhaka: when the breath is held after inhaling it is known as Antara Kumbhaka or Internal Retention.

   2. Bahya Kumbhaka: when the breath is held on exhaling it is known as Bahya Kumbhaka or External Retention.

B. Mechanism-based

1. Sahita Kumbhaka: it is the deliberate stopping of breath, either after inhalation or exhalation, in which conscious effort is involved.

2. Kewal Kumbhaka: when, in the course of practice, the pause persists without effort or discomfort, unconditioned by place, time and number, it is the Kewal Kumbhaka, the absolute and pure pause. This Kumbhaka cures diseases and promotes longevity.

Sahita Kumbhaka

In the Hatha Yogic tradition, pranayama is synonymous with Kumbhaka, or holding the breath after inhalation. **Certain precautions have to be taken to make this type of Kumbhaka safe for the practitioner.** It is essential to be able to deal with the increased pressure inside the chest cavity and the abdomen, so as to maintain it for a longer time without adverse effects. The traditional techniques available to prolong the pauses safely are called bandhas or locks. They have to be learnt under the able guidance of a trained master, and will not be dealt with in this book.

Kewal Kumbhaka – a Blessing for All

It is the spontaneous and comfortable stopping of breath for some time. This is the ultimate aim of pranayama. During Kewal Kumbhaka, the breathing cycle comes to a standstill, with a fully conscious and aware mind. This state is also known as the 'perfectly peaceful pause' or one of complete rest. Feelings such as urgency, motive, desire, anxiety, fear, hatred, anger, and even hunger and thirst will disappear when we are in this state.

Physiologically, it allows better and complete exchange of gases in the lungs with a resultant positive impact on all the functions of the body. Research has shown that by holding the breath during pranayama, metabolic processes in the body decrease in intensity, and the body's consumption of oxygen is reduced to some extent. This means that while holding our breath, our body slows the metabolism and uses the energy conserved in some other way. With this kind of pranayama we also influence the Parasympathetic Nervous System, lowering the heart rate and the blood pressure.

The 'pause' is an extremely powerful technique for evoking the relaxation response. We can attain mental relaxation through these spontaneous pauses. We cannot retain our breathing for an extended duration if we are agitated, nervous, anxious or fatigued.

Let us quickly recollect what we have read about the correlation between our mental state and our breathing – agitated thoughts produce rapid, coarse and erratic breathing, while a calm and composed mind is reflected in slow and smooth breathing. By consciously slowing down the breathing rate, the harmful speed of pointless thoughts comes under control and ultimately, with the spontaneous cessation of breathing, the mind can experience perfect calm, poise and balance – a near thoughtless state of mind, the optimum state for health and healing.

This state of utter blissfulness is within the reach of one and all. The experience of Kewal Kumbhaka is addictive in a good way – physically, mentally, emotionally and spiritually. If practised regularly, this exercise is more relaxing than a cup of coffee or a cigarette. The experience of Kewal Kumbhaka can help gain control, especially in people who are overanxious or have perverted mental tendencies, eventually leading to violence, abuse and addiction.

Methods of experiencing Kewal Kumbhaka, the perfectly peaceful pause

1. **Kapalabhati and Bhastrika:** We can prepare for spontaneous peaceful pauses with breathing practices that supply an excess of oxygen, because the length of time over which a pause may be prolonged without discomfort depends on the supply of oxygen available. Practices like Kapalabhati and Bhastrika (Chapter 15) are used primarily to wash out carbon dioxide from the system but in that process there is an excess

supply of oxygen. This delays the triggering of breaths – a function mediated by chemoreceptors in the brain – thus giving rise to the peaceful pause.

2. **By deliberately slowing down the natural state of breathing**: Rishi Patanjali defines this in his Yoga Sutra as, '*Tasmin sati shwasa – praswasha-yorgati-vicchedah pranayamah.*' (PYS 2:49).

Translated, it means, 'Pranayama means control over the normal pattern of breathing, with a slowing down of the normal pattern of breathing (*vicchedah*), leading ultimately to its total and spontaneous silencing.'

Thus, forceful retention of the breath is not the only way of experiencing the Kewal Kumbhaka. Mere slowing down the rate of normal breathing, and maintaining its rhythm and smoothness with deeper breaths can lead to the above state.

3. **After long-term practice of the Sahita Kumbhaka**: The Yoga Sutra says, '*Bahya abyantara-stambha-vrittir-dishakala sankhyabhih paridrishto divgha sukshmah.*" (11.50).

Translated, it means, 'The breathing movement can come to a standstill in three ways: *Bahya* (after exhaling), *Abhyantara* (after inhaling), and *Stambha* (either way in between, when the breath stops spontaneously after a long-term practice of the earlier two types).'

The *Hathapradipika* (yogic text on Hatha Yoga) states that one has to practise many rounds of Sahita Kumbhaka daily over a long period, and maintain the Kumbhaka state for an increasingly longer time. This will progressively require less physical effort until the stage of Kewal Kumbhaka is reached.

When we begin with pranayama practices we must not try to hold our breath forcefully, but should instead breathe naturally and smoothly. Only after a considerable time, when we have mastered the basic breathing exercises and have no contraindications, can we proceed with voluntary breath-holding (Sahita Kumbhaka) and that too, under the guidance of a

teacher. One is eligible for voluntary breath-holding if one has
the ability to double the duration of exhalation for a long time
with ease and comfort.

Breath retention exercises must be done when we reach the stage
where we have improved our ability to breathe in and out, and
the exercises do not disturb the breathing-in and breathing-out
pattern. Only when we have emptied ourselves of air can we
take a new breath, and only when we draw the breath in can we
hold it. So, if we do not breathe out fully we cannot hold our
breath.

According to Swami Satchidananda, the eligibility criterion for
Sahita Kumbhaka is one's ability to maintain with ease a ratio of
10:20 seconds between inhalation and exhalation.

Pranayama vs. Deep-breathing

Many regard pranayama as deep-breathing, but fundamentally
the two are different.

	PRANAYAMA	DEEP-BREATHING
When	One is relaxed.	Happens secondary to muscular exercise, or is done consciously to overcome fatigue.
Aims at	Balancing the functions of the Autonomic Nervous System, creating psycho-physiological harmony through conscious control of the cerebral cortex.	Providing more oxygen, ridding the body of accumulated CO_2, and overcoming the oxygen debt.
Breathing rate	Slow, aims at slowing down more and more with practice.	Fast when secondary to exercise, and moderate during conscious breathing.

	PRANAYAMA	DEEP-BREATHING
Importance of prolonging exhalation	Yes	No
Heart rate and BP	Are reduced.	Are increased after exercise, and reduced with conscious breathing.
Phases	Three distinct phases, Pooraka, Kumbhaka and Rechaka make one cycle.	Only deep inhalations and exhalations.
Retention	Yes	No
Ratios	Followed to make it rhythmic and stay in control.	No
Techniques to prolong exhalations	Yes. One nostril: AV pranayama narrowed passage: Ujjayi Pran Chanting: Bhramari	No
Bandhas	Yes	No
Attitude	With awareness	More mechanical
ANS	Towards PNS	Towards SNS after exercise.

14

Starting Pranayama

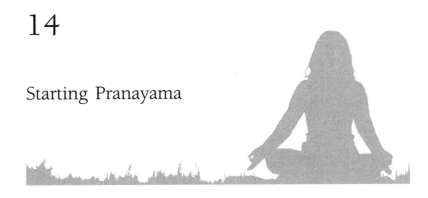

We learn to do something by doing it. There is no other way.

—John Holt

The journey to health

Pranayama Today

After years of remaining in the background, pranayama has now gained popularity. As awareness about its benefits spreads, more and more people are opting for pranayama in an attempt to enjoy better health. It is not uncommon to see people practising it in gardens, on the beach, or even while travelling in a railway compartment.

Every coin has two sides, and while pranayama has immense benefits, there can be ill effects if it is done without proper guidance. It is easy to talk about pranayama, and inhalations and exhalations, but it has to be done correctly to be effective.

Incorrect Practices: Pranayama has to be learnt from a teacher who not only knows the techniques but who can also supervise and correct till one is on the right track. This will differ according to a person's age, breathing ability, disease state, and other important factors. Faulty techniques can do more harm than good, and have to be individually rectified.

Over-enthusiasm: Overdoing pranayama without accepting one's limitations can be dangerous. Using too much force while breathing, struggling to continue a practice for a particular period of time, gasping for air during intervals – these are signs that we are going overboard. Many of us begin pranayama in middle age or mature adult life, when the back is stiff, the knees are arthritic, and the breathing capacity is very restricted. It is always safer to start slowly, progress gradually under guidance, and grow.

Mechanical Attitude: For some, pranayama is a breathing exercise where, by hook or by crook, 'x' pranayama has to be done for 'y' time, followed by 'c' pranayama for 'd' time, and so on. Intent on completing the protocol for the day, we jump from one to the next without being aware of the effects on the body and the mind. Little do we realize how far- reaching, profound and subtle the effects of pranayama can be on our 'monkey mind' in which the roots of most of our problems lie.

When learning pranayama, it is advisable to attend small group sessions or a class where breathing can be monitored. It is the duty of the teacher to give timely instructions and make the necessary corrections.

Posture

Just as a musician prepares for a performance, we too, have to fine-tune ourselves to set a mood for a good practice. Correct posture is indispensable for the successful practice of pranayama. As physical discomfort and mental chatter are closely interrelated, a stable and calm body is a prerequisite for calming the mind. The body has to be kept still and comfortable.

Unnecessary movement dissipates prana so one must be able to sit comfortably in a position for a long period of time. The posture has to be stable (*sthira*) so that minimal effort is required to maintain it. It has to be comfortable (*sukha*) so that it can be maintained, with the mind free from all distractions.

Sitting straight means aligning and balancing the spine along a vertical axis ascending from the base to the skull. Distortions of the spine are not only uncomfortable but, on a very subtle level, block the flow of energy.

The suggested yogic postures are sitting postures with legs crossed in different ways, offering a firm triangular base to the spine, where the spine is erect and all the body parts are relaxed, and which can be mastered under the practical guidance of a yoga teacher – Padmasana (full lotus), Ardhapadmasana (half lotus), Siddhasana, Swastikasana, and Sukhasana (simple cross-legged sitting).

Physiological Advantages of Cross-legged Postures

These postures offer the following important advantages required for meditation:

1. With legs crossed, the posture offers a broad base, a triangular foundation for stability, and allows you to sit comfortably for a long time. They enable the trunk to stay erect so that the natural curves of the spine are maintained without distortion. The head, the neck, the chest and the abdomen are in perfect alignment so that the muscles required for breathing can play freely. These poses prevent the body from collapsing forward, stooping, or tilting to either side. A minimum energy is required for maintaining the posture..

2. The spine is erect in these positions, allowing all the physiological activities to go on smoothly. Physiology says that erect postures create a proper balance for the digestive organs, the heart and the lungs, which can, then, function at optimum level, resulting in increased efficiency and reduced stress.

3. The brain has to work less to keep balance in these positions. Gravity and anti-gravity muscles need not work hard to maintain the pose since the firm triangular base provided by the crossed legs is enough. Closing the eyes is also possible without losing balance.

4. The abdominal muscles, the diaphragm and the muscles in the chest are stressed to the minimum extent. Production of carbon dioxide is minimized, hence, the process of breathing is minimized, and the continuous movement of the diaphragm and the ribs does not disturb the meditative state.

5. These positions are such that the brain and the nervous system are under minimal stress, and the mind can be peaceful, yet alert and relaxed.

6. Only the supine position, that is, the lying-down position, is more relaxed than the meditative position, but there is always a possibility of falling asleep in a horizontal position.

7. The pelvic region (the lower trunk) gets a rich supply of blood, resulting in the toning of the nerves coming from the sacral (the lower part of the spinal cord) region. This increases the balance towards the Parasympathetic Nervous System, thereby easing and releasing stress.

8. The blood from the legs can reach the heart easily, reducing the effort of the heart and the lungs.

9. Yoga psycho-physiology says that the erect spine position offers the least resistance to pranic energy, which is awakened through the meditation and travels up to the brain.

If You Cannot Sit in these Poses

As most of us suffer from habitual muscular stiffness and weakness in the back, legs or shoulders, sitting straight is not as simple as it sounds.

• With rounded and hunched-up shoulders, it is difficult to straighten the upper back and to expand the chest.

• If the lower back is stiff or if the leg muscles are tight, the natural curvature of the lower back gets distorted, collapsing the lower back. This rounds the upper back and pushes it forward to counterbalance the feeling of falling backward.

• While attempting to sit straight, the lower back sometimes gets overarched. This pushes the pelvis forward, creating tension in the spine, the hips and even the neck. It can cause pain below the shoulder blades.

Many of us may also find it difficult to sit in a meditative pose for a long period because we are not habituated to sitting cross-legged. If the bodily discomfort becomes a reason for distraction, we do not get any benefit out of the practice of pranayama. The mind gets diverted towards the discomfort instead of enjoying the subtle effects of pranayama. The aim is not to sit in Padmasana, but to sit so comfortably that one forgets the body and can delve deep into the subtler aspects. Posture and sitting problems should not be a reason for avoiding the practice of pranayama.

WRONG POSTURE

Vajrasana - wrong - rounded back

Vajrasna - wrong - arched back

Wrong sitting on floor

Wrong sitting on chair

Here are a few tips on how to make the posture more comfortable and stable:

1. Sit cross-legged or in half-Padmasana with a cushion under the tail bone. This slight elevation of the spine releases the tension around the hip joints and the thighs, and compensates for limited flexibility while restoring the natural curves of the back. The abdomen also gets a slight lift so that the belly can move freely during the various practices.

2. Sit in Vajrasana with a cushion under the ankles. If necessary, use another cushion between the legs and the thighs. This reduces the strain on the knees and the ankles.

3. Those with old injuries, or extreme stiffness of the knees, the hips or the back, will find sitting on a chair a viable alternative since it enables them to maintain a steady and comfortable posture with a straight spine.

Use a chair with a firm and flat surface, and with a firm back set at a ninety-degree angle to the seat. Sit slightly forward on it, feet uncrossed and flat on the floor, toes pointing in front. The height of the chair should be such that the hips are at a slightly higher level than the knees. As the thighs gently slope forward, the strain in the legs gets minimized. Use a cushion to raise the height of the seat if necessary.

CORRECT POSTURE

Vajrasana - Right sitting

Vajrasana - right with 1 cushion

Vajrasana - right with 2   Correct sitting on chair with
cushions   cushion

Dos and Dont's

For healthy progress in pranayama, some preliminary
preparation will do us good:

• Answer the call of nature before you begin the exercises,
unless you are accustomed to doing it at a later time. If the
bowels are constipated, drink warm water on waking up, do
asanas like Bhujangasana, Shalabhasana, and Dhanurasana. With
regular practice of asanas and pranayama, the natural rhythm
will get established.

• Practise pranayama in a well-ventilated room, in the
balcony, on the terrace, the lawn or the garden. Do not do it in a
closed, air-conditioned room where fresh air is restricted.

• Do not practise pranayama on a full stomach; wait for at
least three hours after a meal. The best time to do pranayama is
early morning. Drink a little fruit juice or a small cup of tea or
coffee, and wait for thirty minutes or so before starting
pranayama.

• Do not practise pranayama if you are very hungry.

- You may drink a cup of milk or eat a light snack ten–fifteen minutes after completing pranayama.

- Wear comfortable and loose clothes. If practising outdoors, cover the body with a loose sheet to avoid disturbance from insects.

- Pranayama needs concentration and attention; do not practise it in distracting company.

- Switch off the mobile phone, the TV, the radio, the call bell and the telephone to avoid distraction.

- Keep a special place for the daily practice, one with minimal disturbances, such as the puja room, the living room, or a special corner in a room. Avoid practising sitting on the bare floor.

- For greater benefit, avoid smoking and drinking, and if possible, opt for a *satvik* diet.

- Be regular and systematic in the practice of pranayama. Missing pranayama should be like missing food. Practising in fits and starts will not impart much benefit. After learning from a trained yoga teacher, one should continue regular practice at home.

- Stop the practice during a sickness like active infections, fever, loose motions, etc.

- If possible, bathe with normal tap water before yogic practices, as it is refreshing and stimulating, it dispels drowsiness, and brings about equilibrium in the blood circulation. Avoid bathing for half an hour after you finish pranayama.

While Practising

- Do some physical practice before doing pranayama to dispel the early morning drowsiness. If you have sufficient time, practise pranayama after doing asanas, Surya Namaskaar, or taking a morning walk.

• Do not use 'lack of time for preliminary exercises' as an excuse to skip pranayama. You can do pranayama without any preliminary exercise too, but remember, maintenance of the body is impossible without asanas or any kind of physical exercise or activity.

• Avoid all strain during pranayama. If you contort the facial muscles during a practice it means that you are going beyond your capacity.

• Never be in a hurry. Practise pranayama with a relaxed mind. This will help you have better control of your breathing. After each exercise, enjoy and appreciate its beneficial effects, and then move on to the next one.

• Too much is bad. Progress slowly and steadily. Do not be in a hurry to get more benefits by increasing the duration of the practice.

• You should feel fresh and joyful after pranayama. If tired and exhausted, reduce the duration or check for other reasons for the fatigue.

• In the beginning, you can mentally keep count of the exercises; later you will not need to be distracted because the lungs will tell you when the required number is done.

• Do not expect benefits in a few days. You need to do at least fifteen minutes of daily practice in the beginning to see results.

• Do not shake the body unnecessarily during practice as this dissipates energy. The posture should be comfortable, steady and firm.

• Aim not just for physical benefits but spiritual progress too. Feel the healthy attributes of peace, joy, compassion, and forgiveness coming in while inhaling; during exhalation feel all the negative qualities of anger, worry, greed and lust dissipating.

• Acknowledge the deep power that underlies each breath. Feel the body getting energized and light with each inhalation, and nurture the attitude of surrender to the cosmic forces as you exhale.

• Use common sense throughout the practice. If one kind of practice is not agreeable to your system, change or avoid it after consulting your teacher. This is called *yukti*.

'Where there is *yukti* (common sense), there is *siddhi, bhukti* and *mukti* (perfection, enjoyment and salvation).'

—Swami Shivanada

Special Guidelines for Beginners

Anyone can benefit from pranayama by following some basic rules. As long as we pay attention to the reactions of the body, there is nothing to fear. Problems can arise when we alter the breathing and are unable to recognize or attend to a negative bodily reaction.

1. Learn pranayama from a compassionate yoga teacher who will guide you and rectify your practice. Be sincere, regular and systematic when practising on your own. You will undoubtedly get success and move towards good health, vitality, peace and joy.

2. To start with, you must practise muscle-stretching and deep-breathing exercises. This helps increase lung volume, reduce tightness of underused muscles, and develop breath and body awareness.

3. People suffering from chronic shortness of breath and conditions like emphysema, bronchitis and asthma should not directly begin pranayama. Practise some asanas first to increase the volume of the lungs, and to free the muscles of the ribs, the back and the diaphragm. Special breathing exercises and deep breathing are a prerequisite to pranayama.

4. The biggest problem that we encounter is the tendency to push ourselves beyond our limit. By pushing too hard we harm ourselves more than we benefit from the practice, and consequently lose interest and give it up altogether. By

proceeding slowly and carefully, we not only make it a pleasurable routine, but also benefit from it.

5. Many of us struggle to breathe deeply as we are generally not used to breathing that way. Some feel an urge to take a quick breath between their long slow breaths. There should be no struggle while breathing. Avoid jerky breathing and take short breaths in between if necessary; the point is to be comfortable.

6. If we experience difficulty in breathing out, or if the quality of exhalation is not good, the entire pranayama practice gets adversely affected. Practising belly-breathing will help overcome this issue (See 'Conscious Breathing')

7. Pranayama and breathing exercises should not be pushed to the extent of weariness and exhaustion.

8. There should be no hurry or haste while performing the exercises. Complete attention should be given to the practice while it is being performed.

9. Do not attempt to hold the breath with force or struggle. Allow the spontaneous pauses or the Kewal Kumbhaka as discussed in the previous chapter.

10. Practice should be meaningfully, not mechanically, performed.

11. Make a few changes in the order of the exercises to break the monotony.

12. Practice should be gentle and non-violent. Breathing should not be jerky or irregular, but smooth, steady and continuous.

As long as we can breathe we can do yoga, which includes asanas and pranayama. Let us, therefore, incorporate this practice in our daily routine under the supervision of a compassionate and understanding teacher.

Yogic lore is a treasure house of many pranayamic practices. We will consider the basic ones that are potent enough to give us what we are expecting out of them – health and vitality both of the body and the mind.

The order in which we proceed is important because no progress ever takes place haphazardly. When we decide to change the furniture in a room, we proceed by first removing the old items, getting the new ones in and then arranging them properly in the room – cleansing, receiving and organizing.

The same is the case with us – we need to first cleanse the body and the mind of the toxins and waste products to create more room for prana, the vital energy we need, which then has to get properly redistributed to different parts. The pranayamic practice should thus follow this sequence:

1. Cleansing breaths: Kapalabhati, Bhastrika

2. Energizing breaths: Anuloma Viloma Nadi Shuddhi (alternate-nostril breathing), Ujjayi breathing

3. Balancing breaths: Bhramari (honey bee sound) and OM chanting

As there is a reason for everything we do, it is important that we first understand the logic behind 'Why I should do this', before we actually begin practising pranayama. This book will satisfy your logical reasoning so that you are convinced, and can then proceed with pranayama, ready to receive, and receive more!

15

Cleansing Breaths –
Kapalabhati and Bhastrika

I heard the sea and asked, 'What language is that?'
The sea replied, 'The language of eternal questions.'
I saw the sky and asked, 'What holds the answer?'
The sky replied, 'The language of eternal silence.'

—Rabindranath Tagore

The process is to stand aside and watch the working of the
Divine Power in yourself.

—Sri Aurobindo

*Exercises to cleanse the body and the mind and bring instant peace
and clarity*

Kapalabhati and Bhastrika are breathing techniques used
primarily for cleansing. They help cleanse the air passage of
mucous, the chest of a sensation of tightness, the lungs of carbon
dioxide, and the mind of a sensation of heaviness and blockage.
Kapalabhati and Bhastrika are versatile breathing techniques of
purification, called *kriya* in yogic terminology. Since they are
breathing practices, many refer to them as pranayama.

We often realise that twenty-four hours are not enough to do the
myriad things we want to do. Time is always short and we need
instant gratification through a quick cup of tea, fast food, and
ready-to-eat snacks. We are always looking for quick fixes,
knowing fully well that the real joy lies inside us; the problem is

in accessing it at our will.

How would you like to experience 'Instant Peace of Mind' with simple techniques of breathing? Here are two methods: the first involves a quick, short, forced exhalation using the abdominal muscles, followed by a slower automatic diaphragmatic inhalation as the abdominal muscles are relaxed; the other is active chest inhalation and exhalation by forced, rapid, deep breathing.

Cleansing the Body

Kapalabhati and Bhastrika are practised mainly to remove impurities from the body as both are based on active exhalations. Our day-to-day breaths are usually shallow with short exhalations, promoting accumulation of the toxic gas, carbon dioxide, in the lungs. These cleansing breaths promote active exhalation, primarily encouraging better removal of carbon dioxide from the lungs. Since the gas is the end product of metabolism in the body, this action indirectly facilitates removal of tissue or body toxins as well.

Cleansing the Mind

These practices have a unique effect on the mind, too. During the active phase of the practice, they stimulate the brain cells to get invigorated by favourably influencing the oxygen and carbon dioxide balance. In the process, not only is there a washing out of carbon dioxide from the system but also a greater supply of oxygen. This delays the triggering of the breath – a function mediated by chemoreceptors (special cells in the brain sensitive to low levels of oxygen in blood). Due to greater levels of oxygen in the blood, the chemoreceptors relax, and the triggering of the breath is delayed for some time, resulting in a peaceful pause in breathing.

When breathing comes to this temporary standstill (Kewal Kumbhaka), we are aware that the mind is in a very calm and balanced state that rejuvenates and heals. Thus we can prepare for spontaneous peaceful pauses with practices that supply excess of oxygen, because the length of time for which a pause may be prolonged without discomfort depends on the supply of oxygen available.

Kapalabhati (Cleansing Breaths)

Kapalabhati is literally 'that which shines or brings a glow to the forehead – *kapaal*. In Sanskrit, kapaal means skull or forehead, and *bhati* means luminosity and perception. Kapalabhati is the practice that brings a state of luminousness or clarity, in the mind as well as the body by

- cleansing the nasal passageway and the sinuses

- removing carbon dioxide gas which is toxic to body and mind

- supplying the brain with fresh oxygen-rich blood

It is essentially a voluntary abdominal breathing practice with the focus on forceful exhalations. In normal breathing, inhalation is active while exhalation is passive. In Kapalabhati, exhalation is active while inhalation is passive. It is done in quick succession with the help of the abdominal muscles, while the chest is more or less quiet and unmoving. The abdominal muscles are made to contract actively and with force, so that the forceful upward movement of the diaphragm expels the air. The diaphragm then descends easily, creating a slight reduction in the pressure in the lungs, and the atmospheric air rushes in. A blowing sound is produced during the active exhalation, while the passive inhalation is a silent one.

Kapalbhati - blowing technique for beginners

Kapalabhati is a rapid diaphragmatic breathing that cleanses and energizes. It is the kriya that cleanses the respiratory tract and destroys all mucous disorders. Broadly speaking, it stimulates an all-round activity in the body. It expels the stagnant air in the lower lobes of the lungs (which remains there due to shallow breathing). It also clears out the air passage, the lungs and the nostrils. Kapalabhati is the ideal exercise when we feel heavy or foggy in the head, or experience a feeling of heaviness around the eyes or sinuses.

With the practice of Kapalabhati the lungs are cleansed of carbon dioxide – the toxic end product of metabolism. The toxins and the acidic residues in the body tissues, that are the end product of metabolism, get converted to carbonic acid ($H_2 Co_3$), which breaks up into water and carbon dioxide. This carbon dioxide is exhaled actively via the lungs. So, Kapalabhati not only cleanses the lungs, but also rids the tissues and the blood of toxic waste products, most of which ultimately get converted to carbon dioxide. This brings a sense of lightness in the body and alertness in the mind. The practice brings a glow to the crown and lightness to the brain; hence the name Kapalabhati.

Technique

• Sit in a comfortable pose, spine erect, and maintain its natural curve. The position must be such that the belly muscles are relaxed and able to move freely and actively, keeping the body steady and comfortable.

• Place your palms on the thighs or knees. This helps lift the spine and pushes the shoulders back.

• Relax the nose and soften the face with a gentle smile.

• Begin with a chest-expanding inhalation and, maintaining it, start the practice. Use your abdominal muscles to perform active forceful exhalations, followed by passive soundless inhalations. Breathe only through the nose.

• During exhalation, push out the air with a strong flapping movement of the abdomen in an upward direction. At the end of each exhalation, allow the abdominal muscles to relax as the inhalations happen passively, recoiling from the force of exhalation. Inhalation is smooth and effortless, and prepares the practitioner for the next thrust of the abdomen.

• A correct practice of Kapalabhati produces a crisp sound as one exhales without any facial contortions. The sound is produced by the volume of air being pushed up by the forceful action of the diaphragm, not of the muscles of the chest, the shoulders, the neck or the face.

• The rate: To start with, do ten–twenty expulsions per round, at a rate of one second for exhalation and two-three seconds for the inhalation, resting between the rounds. You can gradually increase the speed and the number of expulsions to about sixty per round (one expulsion per second), resting between rounds till an equilibrium is established. With regular and sustained practice, one can achieve a speed of 100-120 strokes per minute. It is essential not to sacrifice the force of the abdominal contraction to achieve a greater speed.

• The rhythm: Exhalations should be regular and consistent, like the ticking of a clock. Jerky and erratic breaths will lead to hunger for air in the form of intermittent gasping for breath. The rhythm should be slow and steady initially, allowing enough time for spontaneous inhalations to occur.

• The pause: At the end of one round, take a short rest. Sit very still and observe the body and the mind, and experience the feeling of peace. There will be an automatic suspension of breathing. This is called Kewal Kumbhaka. The urge to breathe stops for a few seconds. Simultaneously, the mind experiences a deep state of stillness, silence, calm and peace. Enjoy this state of deep rest and freshness.

• Wait until the breath automatically resumes and then go on to the next round.

• How much you should practise: if you feel fatigued or dizzy, or experience discomfort in the abdomen or the back during the practice, slow down or stop for a while. Stay within your capacity – it is not a competitive activity.

The Magic of the Pause

Kewal Kumbhaka is the reward of Kapalabhati. It is the automatic cessation of breathing due to carbon dioxide debt and oxygen build-up in the respiratory system and the blood. Breathing stops spontaneously for a while and the mind feels peaceful and calm. The density of thoughts significantly reduces during this time, giving the mind some rest.

The breathing gradually becomes normal as the carbon dioxide builds up in the system. The duration of Kumbhaka lengthens if we relax and enjoy it consciously. With practice and time, the duration of this perfectly peaceful pause increases and the level of relaxation rises, while the rate at which the carbon dioxide builds up slows down.

What if ...

• **My stomach protrudes during active exhalation of Kapalabhati?**

This means that you are unknowingly a reverse breather. You must first correct this; follow the technique explained in the earlier section on 'Conscious Breathing'.

• **I feel pressure in my perineum (lower body)?**

If you feel pressure in the perineum during exhalation, it means that your muscular activity is aiming downward rather than upward towards the chest cavity. You can correct this habit by retraining the abdominal muscles to contract upward during normal exhalations, coughing and sneezing. If left uncorrected, it can lead to problems like incontinence.

• **I am unable to learn Kapalabhati?**

Sit erect and hold up your index finger at arm's length from the body. Pretend that you are blowing out a candle. Lo and behold! Your belly goes in as you blow! This short burst of air employs the same force that you need for Kapalabhati. Continue blowing in a rhythmic way through your mouth and observe the flapping movement of your belly. As you continue blowing, shut your mouth and continue this same pattern of breathing through your nose. That is how you can start doing Kapalabhati.

• **I do not feel the pause when I stop?**

It means you are not giving enough time for inhalations between your active exhalations. You might find yourself gasping for breath. Reduce the rate of your strokes, thereby allowing passive in-breaths.

Precautions

• This exercise should be performed preferably early in the morning and that too, on an empty stomach to avoid digestive disorders. If you plan to perform it after a meal, maintain a gap of at least two to three hours between the meal and the practice of Kapalabhati.

• Avoid wrong postures such as a slouched back, forward-drooping shoulders or a hunched upper back, all of which could lead to muscle spasms and pain in the back or the neck. Do not contract the face or squeeze the nostrils. A smile on the face and a calm demeanour will make the practice easy and pleasurable.

• Do not lift the shoulders with each breath.

• Keep the chest expanded and immobile as the breathing is due to active abdominal muscles at work.

• Stop and rest if any sensations of dizziness or light-headedness occur during rapid breathing.

• Women should avoid doing this exercise during menstruation or pregnancy.

• Kapalabhati is to be avoided by anyone suffering from uncontrolled or severe hypertension, active heart disease, vertigo, glaucoma, a bleeding nose, fluid in the ears, epilepsy, hernia, reflex oesophagitis, a gastric ulcer, or a slipped disc.

Benefits

• Energizes and rejuvenates the body, dispelling lethargy and drowsiness.

• Invigorates the brain cells, improving memory and comprehension. Increases the circulation of blood with higher oxygen concentration, thus revitalizing the brain to function better.

• Regular practice detoxifies the body and brightens up the face.

• Strengthens the nervous system.

• Strengthens and makes the abdominal muscles flexible.

• Massages the abdominal organs, benefiting people with digestive problems.

• Helps rid the lungs of stale residual air resulting from the habit of shallow breathing. Simultaneously, it increases the oxygen concentration in the lungs.

• Cleanses the lungs and the entire respiratory system, increases the lung and the respiratory capacity, benefiting people suffering from respiratory disorders.

• Increases the heart rate, the pumping of blood throughout the body. Improves cellular functioning since more oxygen is available to the cells.

• Increases metabolism, hence, is beneficial for diabetics and obese people.

• Helps relieve backache, which is caused not just by weak muscles but also the weak abdominal wall compounded with a protruding belly. A distended abdomen pulls the back forward, distorting the spinal alignment and stretching the back-muscles, resulting in a spasm. Kapalabhati helps relieve backache by strengthening the muscles of the back and the abdomen, improving the posture, and relieving mental stress

• Purifies the blood, resulting in a lustrous skin.

• Keeps the mind from distracting thoughts and prepares it for better functioning and meditation. Kewal Kumbhaka, the automatic cessation of breath, gives instant peace to the mind. This restful state allows the mind to work with focus and clarity. It helps in decision-making, and allows objectivity and creativity.

• Promotes mental well-being since negative thoughts are thrown out while exhaling.

Physiological Effects

• The volume of air taken in during this breathing is only 150-200 ml per breath. However, the total air taken per minute is more than normal due to the higher rate of breathing.

• Due to the increased work of breathing, the oxygen consumption also increases by 10-40 per cent.

• Since large quantities of carbon dioxide get washed out, the respiratory centre does not get stimulated for breathing, thereby allowing the pause and inducing a tranquil state of mind.

• The heart rate increases slightly by fifteen–twenty beats per minute, and the systolic blood pressure increases by 7-10 mm hg. The diastolic blood pressure remains more or less the same.

• There is a slight increase in the sympathetic tone in the body, followed by a parasympathetic predominance after the practice. The result is a balance between the sympathetic and the parasympathetic, and brings about a feeling of relaxation.

Bhastrika (Bellows)

Bhastrika means bellows, a device with an air bag that emits a stream of air when squeezed together with two handles, used by a blacksmith for blowing air into a fire while working on iron. Bhastrika consists basically of forced, rapid, deep breathing. We use our chest as bellows to get active inhalations and exhalations. Although air is forced both in and out, more emphasis is placed upon the expulsion of air. The practice promotes increase in lung ventilation, blood circulation, clearing of the nasal tract, and increased thinking capacity.

Beginners should limit their practice to about five-ten expulsions. Dizziness is a signal to stop the practice. Beginners are also advised to increase the depth of their breaths with time and patience. The guiding motive in doing this practice should be comfort. Caution should be exercised about the temptation to overdo it, which may bring on dizziness, light-headedness and drowsiness. Overdoing the exercise is contraindicated, but if you feel drowsy, lie down and allow the breathing pattern to rectify itself. Avoid unsupervised excesses to prevent injury to lung tissues.

Technique

• Sit in a comfortable posture (Vajrasana, cross-legged position) with the spine erect. Sitting promotes relaxation of the abdominal muscles, and easy diaphragmatic breathing.

• Relax the body and mind with a gentle smile.

• Breathe by expanding and compressing the chest like a bellows, so that both inhalations and exhalations are active. Bhastrika is thoracic chest-breathing, unlike Kapalabhati, which involves active abdominal exhalations, followed by passive inhalations.

• Initially the rate of breathing has to be slow; start with five–ten and progress slowly under supervision.

• After the final expulsion inhale as deeply as possible. Then slowly, exhale as deeply as possible. The end of this deep exhalation completes one round of Bhastrika.

• The breath stops on its own; enjoy the cessation and the calmness that results (Kewal Kumbhaka).

• Rest a while after one round is over. Take a few normal breaths. This will give you relief and make you fit for the second round.

• Do at least three rounds in the morning, and three in the evening.

- With practice, you can increase the rate to 120 strokes per minute. It is more important to breathe completely with concentration rather than aim for a faster rate with shallow breaths.

- Reduce the duration if you feel giddy or light-headed, or else practise a modified, safer version that includes shrugging the shoulders with the breaths.

Modified Technique for Beginners

The body takes time to adjust to the rapid alterations in carbon dioxide levels, and beginners may experience light-headedness or giddiness when they start Bhastrika. A simpler version is to practise active breathing with shoulder-shrugging.

Sit comfortably with the spine erect and place your palms on your thighs or knees. Raise the shoulders towards the ears with the inhalation, and bring them down with the exhalation. The rhythm of the breath has to coordinate with the rhythm of the shoulder shrugs.

Overall, the precautions and the benefits of Bhastrika are the same as Kapalabhati. Some specific benefits of Bhastrika are:

- It relieves inflammation of the throat.

- Increases gastric fire and improves digestion.

- Helps alleviate diseases of the nose and the chest.

- Improves the appetite.

- Gives more warmth to the body.

Can Kapalabhati and Bhastrika be called pranayama?

Kapalabhati and Bhastrika have two distinct functions: the first is the cleansing aspect or the kriya where the carbon dioxide is getting pumped out, and the second is the pranayama part where Kewal Kumbhaka sets in, followed by a slowing down of the breaths. The duration of Kewal Kumbhaka decides whether the practice is acting as a kriya or a pranayama. If it is sufficiently long (thirty seconds to one minute of active practice), then it is pranayama.

Why does the mind feel calm with these practices?

Kapalabhati clears the respiratory and the nasal passages, massages the abdominal organs, and stimulates digestion, at the same time enhancing concentration by improving the blood flow to the brain. On a deeper level, it clears the mind and sets the stage for pranayama and meditation. Although the action takes place in the abdomen, the subtler effects can be felt in the mind. We can perceive the kapaal, the forehead, like we never have before – without the usual rush of thoughts!

The chaotic speed of our erratic thoughts is reflected immediately on our breaths. So with spontaneous breath control, or the pause that follows these practices, we are able to experience the 'reduced mental chatter' as mental calm and inner peace. Kapalabhati and Bhastrika are thus techniques for experiencing 'instant peace of mind'.

We all go through patches in life when we are indecisive, agitated, or disturbed. Kapalabhati can be practised for a few minutes as an emergency tool to tap the inner voice for guidance. The peace that one experiences during the pause gives a deep rest to the mind, which is overtired with our incessant mental chatter. This rest rejuvenates the mind, helps it to perform better, and subsequently, gives us balanced answers to our problems.

Research substantiates these effects. According to studies, exercises like Bhastrika and Kapalabhati lead to excitation of the Central Nervous System (CNS). This voluntary hyperventilation (increased breathing) induces increased arousal and anxiety. The reduced carbon dioxide concentration in the blood is a key physiological factor underlying these effects. The subjective experience is one of stimulation followed immediately by relaxation. The mechanism probably also involves stimulation of visceral (pertaining to the organs in the abdomen) nerves that stimulate the Parasympathetic Nervous System to ease and release stress, and its effects.

16

Swara Yoga – The Science of Nasal Breath

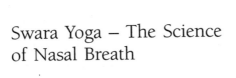

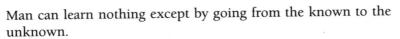

Man can learn nothing except by going from the known to the unknown.

—Claude Bernard

How the nasal cycle and body rhythms affect health.

With an increased awareness of our breathing, we will observe that, at a particular time, there is a difference in the flow of air in our two nostrils. At times it seems as if the right nostril is more active, and at others, the left nostril seems to be permitting more free flow of air. Don't panic, this is not abnormal. In fact, it is a normal cyclic phenomenon occurring with all of us, and science has now discovered that each nostril switches its breathing dominance every one and a half to two hours. Diseases can be diagnosed when one nostril is dominant continuously because this reflects an imbalance in the system.

Ancient *rishis* evolved a complete science called 'Swara Yoga' around this changing flow of breath in the nostrils. They knew that the nostrils are not just the entrance for the air coming in, but are gateways to a vast energy system inside the body. They also knew that the two nostrils function separately and have varying influences on us. 'Swara' means the sound of one's own breath and 'Yoga' means union. Simply said, Swara Yoga enables one to reach the state of union by means of one's own breath.

The rishis observed that this rise and fall of breath also governs many activities of the body, such as the functioning of the internal organs, the onset of disease, and the equanimity or instability of the mind. Ancient yoga writings on Swara Yoga in texts like the *Shiv Swarodaya* claim that the modes of mental activity too, depend on which nostril is dominant or most open to airflow.

Swara Yoga could thus be called the ancient science of natural body rhythms. It explains how the breaths can be manipulated to control the movement of energy, that is prana, thus influencing the functioning of the body and the mind. Modern research in electromagnetic fields and the behaviour of bioenergy has substantiated the vast knowledge on this science of breath.

According to Swara Yoga:

1. **Alternating nostril dominance**: The nostrils alternate in their dominance in a natural and rhythmic way. In a healthy person the breath will alternate between the nostrils every one and a half to two hours.

2. **Left vs. right-nostril breathing and the body functions**: Swara Yoga believes that left-nostril breathing dissipates heat from the body and has a cooling effect. The left nostril is thus called the Chandra (moon) Nadi and is associated with the Ida Nadi, th channel of energy flow that is constructive, anabolic and energy-conserving by nature. The right nostril is called the Surya (sun) Nadi and is associated with the Pingala Nadi, which is catabolic, heat-generating and energy-consuming.

3. Left versus right-nostril breathing and the mind: Certain psychological states of the mind are associated with dominance by a particular nostril:

   • Right-nostril dominance is associated with vigorous activities, an aggressive and competitive nature, and more alertness to external happenings.

   • Left-nostril dominance is related to a quiet and receptive state of mind, with activities of assimilation, creativity and conservation.

4. **An abnormally long dominance of one nostril is an** indication of physical or mental ill health. This time period varies considerably depending on the age, the vitality and the state of health of different persons.

- If the right nostril is overly dominant, the result is mental and nervous disturbances.

- When the left nostril is overly dominant, the result is fatigue and reduced vitality.

Science and Swara Yoga

Medical science has recently discovered the dynamics of the nasal cycle, known to the yogis hundreds of years ago, and accepted that:

- We do not breathe equally through both nostrils.

- It is easier to breathe through one nostril at a particular time.

- This alternates every one and a half to two hours in healthy individuals.

- An abnormally prolonged dominance by one nostril signifies an imbalance and an unhealthy condition.

- The nasal cycle corresponds with the brain functions.

- Imbalances in the nasal cycle are associated with agitation, mood swings, and problems with concentration.

The Nasal Cycle

When we breathe, the nostrils periodically switch dominance; this is known as the nasal cycle. Dr. Kayser, a German physician, first noted the nasal cycle in 1895, and defined it as congestion in one nostril with simultaneous decongestion in the other nostril. Generally, airflow dominates through the decongested nostril for a period, and then congestion and decongestion switch places. This continues through both the waking and the sleeping hours. The average length of a cycle is about two to three hours, and is partly related to age and health.

The physiology was later explained as the interplay of the functioning of the Sympathetic and the Parasympathetic Nervous Systems. Our nostrils are not only densely innervated with the fibres of the Autonomic Nervous System (ANS) but also have a direct connection to the brain and are thus pathways to our mind and body systems. The nostrils are richly endowed with twenty times more autonomic nerve fibres, which connect them to the hypothalamus in the brain. The hypothalamus, along with the ANS, controls the physiological functions and the emotional states of the mind and the body. (Chapter 2)

The dominance of sympathetic activity on one side produces vasoconstriction (narrowing of blood vessels), allowing greater airflow, while the other nostril exhibits a simultaneous dominance of the parasympathetic activity, causing local swelling and thus a restricted airflow.

What governs the nasal cycle?

The Autonomic Nervous System (ANS) modulates the nasal cycle in a rhythmic way. A unique feature of the ANS is that it is designed to work in a natural rhythm of the alternating functions of its two limbs – the Sympathetic and the Parasympathetic Nervous Systems. This rhythm is ultradian in nature, that is, it occurs several times in a twenty-four-hour period.

Secondly, this cyclic nature and the rhythm of the ANS functions are lateralized (on one side of the body). When one branch (SNS) dominates one side of the body, the other branch (PNS) dominates the opposite side, and then the two systems switch dominance in a rhythmic manner.

Autonomic Imbalances and Diseases

Continuous dominance by a particular nostril signifies an imbalance between the active Sympathetic Nervous System (Pingala Nadi) and the healing Parasympathetic Nervous Sytem (Ida Nadi): either should be able to return the body to a state of harmony or homeostasis. When the ability of the body to balance gets deranged, it results in ill health and disease.

Who controls the rhythm of the ANS?

The hypothalamus regulates the ANS to function in a rhythmic manner. Since the hypothalamus is the seat of our emotions it also serves as a neural matrix, a junction point for coupling states of the mind with the body, affecting its metabolism through its control over the ANS. Thus, the hypothalamus is the chief coordinator and, through the ANS, it controls the physiological functions of the body and the emotional states of the mind.

So, the natural rhythmic activity of the ANS is mediated through the hypothalamus leading to the lateralized rhythm (alternating dominance by the SNS and the PNS functions) of the ANS, and also its effects on the organs and the structures that function under the control of the ANS. When sympathetic activity prevails on the left side of the body, parasympathetic prevails on the right, and they keep alternating.

Here are some findings to substantiate the hypothesis:

Lateralized Variation in the Stress Hormone Levels

Catecholamines are the ANS hormones that regulate many body functions. They are secreted in stressful situations upon stimulation of the sympathetic nervous impulses. The levels of these stress hormones have been found to be different in the blood drawn from both sides of the body at the same time. Moreover, the levels of the hormones too, have been found to change and alternate as the nasal dominance changed.

Changing Skin Resistance

A special device was used to gauge the changes in skin resistance in response to a change in local skin temperature. The skin resistance was found to be different on the two sides of the body. The Sympathetic and the Parasympathetic Nervous Systems supply the sweat glands in the body which play an important role in determining the local skin temperature. Alternations in their functions also affect the sweat glands, the local skin temperature, and the local skin resistance. Left-nostril breathing, which is interpreted as a reduction of the sympathetic activity, increased the galvanic skin resistance on the hands, and vice versa.

Nasal Cycle and Alternating Brain Hemisphere Activity

Our brain has two hemispheres or halves that have evolved to complement each other and to balance the functions of life. Each half of the brain performs separate functions. The left side is for our basic knowledge, personal skills, and daily language. It controls our rational and outer directed selves. It deals with logical or linear thinking, verbal and routine memory, logical thought, analytical thinking, and actions that go with our thoughts. The left side helps us decide what to do to meet with our goals or arrive at our destination.

The right half gives us a perspective on our goals in life and our relationships. It controls our inner directed self that deals with intuition, our artistic and creative selves, spatial relationships, visual images, aesthetics and our meditative space. The right half tells us where we are going in life.

Just as the nasal cycle has a rhythm governed by the rhythmic functions of the ANS, there is a rhythm in the functioning of the two hemispheres or halves of the brain. At times, the functions corresponding to the right side of the brain dominate, and at other times, those of the left hemisphere. The unique point to note is that these two rhythms – nasal and cerebral (pertaining to the brain) – are coupled or linked with each other. In other words, the nasal cycle is linked with the rhythm of alternating brain (cerebral) hemispheric activity as well, both during the waking and the sleeping states.

Mental capabilities corresponding to the left hemisphere dominate when the right nostril is more open. Likewise, the right hemispheric mental capabilities dominate when the left nostril dominates. Equal airflow through both the nostrils represents a balance of the two mental modes.

This was interpreted by measuring the changes in the electrical activity of the brain through the changing power in the EEG (electroencephalogram) and 148 channel magneto-encephalography (MEG) studies. Electrical activity was found to be greater on the opposite side of the dominant nostril. When airflow dominated in the right nostril, there was greater cerebral activity in the left hemisphere, and vice versa.

Right nasal dominance was found to be coupled with better verbal performance, which is a left-brain activity, while left nasal dominance was associated with greater spatial skills, a right-brain skill. It is a known fact that the right side of the brain controls creative activity while the left side controls logical and verbal activity.

How are the nasal cycle and brain activities linked?

The nostril that is more active and allows freer flow of air is decongested due to local constriction of blood vessels (a Sympathetic Nervous System function) This increases the sympathetic tone, and produces vasoconstriction in the same-sided brain (because the sympathetic nerve fibres do not cross to the opposite side). This reduces the blood flow and the cortical activity on the same side of the brain.

It has been suggested that increased parasympathetic activity occurs simultaneously in the opposite half of the brain cortex to compensate, thus helping to maintain good blood flow in the total brain. This could be the reason for better cognitive functioning of the opposite side of the brain.

To put it simply ...

• The nasal cycle serves as a unique marker for the lateralized rhythms of the ANS and its functions. It exhibits as an ultradian rhythm (occurring in the hourly range) with greater airflow through one nostril followed by a reversal in the airflow dominance.

• This phenomenon is an alternating congestion and decongestion of opposite nostrils under the influence of the dense fibres of the ANS in the nose. Dominant sympathetic activity on one side produces constriction in the nasal cavity, which is paralleled by vasodilation in the other nostril due to dominant parasympathetic activity. The increased flow of blood in the blood vessels due to an increase in their diameter, leads to local swelling and increases congestion and resistance to airflow. This flow of air shifts from one nostril to the other every one to three hours in a biological rhythm corresponding to the change in the rhythm of the ANS.

• The nasal cycle is an indicator of the alternating rhythm of the Autonomic Nervous System. Since the ANS coordinates all the physiological functions of the body—digestion, circulation and excretion—the nasal cycle has a parallel effect on the various physiological and metabolic functions of the body

• When we breathe more easily through the left nostril, the functioning of the right brain hemisphere is more pronounced and dominant than the left brain hemisphere. Easier breathing through the right nostril, on the other hand, means that the left brain hemisphere is currently dominating. When we can breathe equally through both nostrils there is some kind of balance between the left and the right brain hemisphere functions, throughout the nervous system, our physiology and health. Thus, the nasal cycle and the psychological and cognitive functions of the brain also go hand in hand, changing dominance.

Factors that Can Shift Nasal Dominance

Environment: The dominance of the nostril changes with a change in the environment and the temperature. On a cold winter day, the right nostril is fully open and trying hard to warm the body. When the external temperature suddenly changes, and one walks into an overheated room, the right nostril shuts down and the left nostril takes over.

Mental state: During an afternoon nap, the right nostril is less active, allowing us to rest. If the phone suddenly rings and we wake up from a deep sleep, the left nostril engorges, allowing the right nostril to open so that our logical faculty is activated to be present for the call.

Posture and the physical states: While we are asleep the nostrils shift as we turn from side to side. If we lie on one side, the opposite nostril opens up. Asymmetric or unilateral pressure on the chest, the shoulders, the trunk or the buttocks can shift nasal dominance. It has been found that asymmetrical pressure on the two sides of the chest (when we lie on one side) triggers vasomotor reflexes (interactions between the muscles, the blood vessels and the nerves) that increase nasal resistance on the side of the pressure, and decrease it on the other side. Pressure over a point in the axilla (armpit), approximately over the fifth intercostal (between the ribs) space, can induce increased sympathetic tone on the opposite side of the body. This parallels the ancient yogic observation that, placing a crutch or *yoga-danda* under one arm while upright, leads to same-sided nasal congestion and opposite decongestion.

Implications:

• Nasal dominance can shift due to asymmetrical weight distribution while seated.

• Nasal resistance can become low and nearly symmetrical during exercise.

• Psychological factors such as stress, fear, and frustration can apparently affect nasal resistance.

• The cycle can become erratic with emotional disturbance, irregular eating or sleeping habits, and various other lifestyle factors.

The Nasal Cycle and Diseases

Thanks to continuing research on this subject, we now accept the nasal cycle and its co-relation with several body and mental functions. However, medical science is still catching up with the ancient yogis who went one step ahead, and observed that many diseases were due to a disturbance in the nasal cycle.

According to the concepts of Swara Yoga, if the breath continues to flow through one nostril for more than two hours – as it usually does with most of us – it has an adverse effect on our health in some form or the other. If the right nostril dominates most of the time it will lead to mental and nervous irritability, whereas an overactive left nostril will lead to fatigue and reduced brain functioning. The longer the flow of breath in one nostril, the more serious the outcome is. The yogis developed the alternate-nostril breathing technique to prevent and correct many such body and mental imbalances.

Yogis observed that, if a person breathed too long through one nostril, it could lead to different illnesses. They believed that diabetes was caused, to a large extent, by breathing mainly through the right nostril. They also knew that prolonged breathing only through the left nostril (over a period of years) could produce asthma, but that it could be eliminated by teaching asthmatics to breathe only through the right nostril until the asthma was cured. To prevent a recurrence, they were then taught to practise alternate-nostril breathing.

Modern research has substantiated the benefits of alternate-nostril breathing in various stress-born illnesses, and it is now a part of many health management programmes for ischemic heart disease, asthma, diabetes, etc. The great advantage is that it can be practised by one and all, anywhere, anytime.

Many clinical studies have also pointed out the need for balanced breaths through both nostrils for good health. Dr. I.N. Rega, an ENT specialist from Romania, observed the effects of a deviation of the nasal septum (the partition between the two nostrils) on health. Deviation of the septum to one side leads to a one-sided nasal obstruction. He observed that patients whose breath flowed mainly through the left nostril suffered a higher-than-average incidence of respiratory disorders like sinusitis, ear infection, pharyngitis, tonsillitis, bronchitis, and asthma. They were also more likely to suffer from distant disorders like intellectual weakness, forgetfulness, headaches, menstrual irregularities, etc. Patients whose breath flowed predominantly from the right nostril were predisposed to diabetes, hypertension and its consequences, since breathing mainly through the right nostril stimulates the Sympathetic Nervous System, and consequently causes problems of high blood pressure.

This validates what yogis said way back in time. They not only observed asthma in people who were left-nostril breathers but also advised them to breathe through the right nostril till they were cured of asthma. This concept of single-nostril breathing has been taught for various other physical and mental problems, too. In the event of any illness, be it headache, bodyache, depression or anxiety, the person is asked to breathe through the nostril that is more blocked. This corrects the energy or the pranic imbalance, thereby resetting the inner equilibrium towards health.

Single-nostril Breathing (SNB)

Single-nostril breathing is breathing consciously through one nostril while keeping the other blocked. It is found that **right-nostril breathing** stimulates the left brain hemisphere and the functions of the Sympathetic Nervous System, leading to an accelerated heart rate, higher blood pressure and a greater consumption of oxygen by the body cells. **Left-nostril breathing** stimulates the right brain hemisphere and intensifies the functions of the Parasympathetic Nervous System. Thus, the nasal cycle is an indicator of internal imbalances, and can be modulated to correct the disequilibrium of bodily functions.

• **Headache and Migraine:** Scientists like Nobel Prize-winner Sir John Carew Eccles, and Kitrelle found that the inner balance gets disrupted under stress or with marked hypothalamic instability, resulting in marked autonomic asymmetry that manifests as migraine, cluster headaches and Ménière's disease. This may explain the asymmetrical autonomic response observed in migraine with one-sided headache, flushing, visual distortion and nasal congestion.

• **Diabetes:** A scientist by the name Backon observed and postulated that right-nostril breathing significantly increases blood glucose levels while left-nostril breathing lowers it. This could explain the yogic postulate that diabetes may precipitate when one breathes through the right nostril most of the time.

• **Glaucoma:** Studies have shown that right nostril breathing leads to a 23 per cent reduction in the intraocular (eye) pressure while left-nostril breathing increases it by an insignificant 4.5 per cent.

• **Obsessive Compulsive Disorders:** Dr. David Shannahoff-Khalsa has studied a specific pattern of left-nostril breathing that helps ameliorate the symptoms of Obsessive Compulsive Disorder (OCD), the fourth most common psychiatric disorder, and one of the least controllable by conventional treatment. He believes that those who suffer from OCD have a right-hemispheric defect, which can be corrected by adopting the left-nostril breathing pattern.

• **Autism:** A study done by Dane on autistic children concluded that autism and early language impairment may be associated with left-handedness and left nasal dominance. Patients with autism have an abnormal nasal cycle—probably almost continuous left-nostril breathing.

• **Asthma:** Prolonged breathing from the left nostril over years can produce asthma. Teaching the person to breathe through the right nostril till the asthma gets cured, and then to maintain his health and balance with the alternate-nostril breathing technique can eliminate this. Khanam showed that yoga training for one week decreased sympathetic reactivity in asthma patients and improved lung functions.

• **Breast Cancer:** In studies of breast cancer, differences were found in the sensitivity of the left and the right breast to hormonal stimulation. There is possibly an autonomic correlate as breast cancer gets triggered with stress and bereavement.

- The one-sided stress of ANS functions deserves attention in many common diseases – pneumonia, kidney disease, hyper and hypothyroid conditions, certain tumours, skin rash, and inflammation of the ovaries or testicles, where commonly unilateral or one-sided affliction is observed.

Thus the ANS-CNS rhythm manifests as an internal pendulum of lateralizing activities, and this shift in various body rhythms indicates balance and health (homeostasis). What the yogis viewed as balance of breathing is now more acceptable as a tool for health and harmony. Diseases occur when the internal rhythms are disturbed as indicated by the breathing rhythm that does not shift (the nasal cycle).

Alternate-nostril breathing is a useful tool for one and all as it induces a balance in the ANS-CNS functions, thereby resetting the electrical patterns, the energy dynamics, and the chemical balance. It is a true balance between our metabolism and our awareness. This reduces the stress that is at the root of our problems and ailments.

Dr. David Shannahoff-Khalsa makes a practical suggestion to balance this undue stress on one side of the body and brain:

'If you want to alter an unwanted state, just breathe through the more congested nostril.'

This leads us to a new understanding of ANS-CNS activities and helps define the link between our mental state, the effect on the body, and how the regulation of the nasal cycle can be a tool for influencing the mind-body complex in a beneficial way.

17

Nadi Shuddhi Pranayama – Energy Channel Cleanser

Slow down and enjoy life. It's not only the scenery you miss by going too fast – you also miss the sense of where you are going and why.

—Eddie Cantor

If you do not learn from history, you will have to relive history.

—Marcus Cicero

Self-healing by balancing the breaths

Slow breathing technique, that is, breathing alternately through each nostril, is dynamic in its effects. It has a purifying effect on the energy channels of the body because it unblocks and thus balances the flow of vital energy, prana, by passing the breath alternately through one nostril and then the other.

In this practice, we breathe through one nostril at a time. We know that our normal breathing does alternate from one nostril to the other at different times during the day. In a healthy person this alternation of breath takes place roughly every one and a half to two hours. However, this normal rhythm gets disturbed in most of us, and actually varies considerably, leading to reduced vitality and ill health.

To make the pattern and flow of breath more natural and healthier, we need to regulate and balance our breath. The technique of alternate-nostril breathing was developed to rebalance the equilibrium of breathing, and also the mind. The *nadi shuddhi* pranayama enables self-healing by balancing the Sympathetic and the Parasympathetic Nervous Systems.

Yogic writings use a variety of terms for alternate-nostril breathing – *nadi shodhanam, nadi shuddhi* and *sukha purvaka* pranayama. This exercise cleanses and rejuvenates the vital channels of energy hence the name 'nadi shuddhi pranayama'. It is an exceptionally powerful technique for calming and relaxing the mind and the body.

Alternate-nostril breathing literally means breathing alternately through the two nostrils. It consists of slow, deep, quiet breathing, using one nostril at a time. Each breath is as slow and as comfortable, using full lung capacity, as in the complete breath. The thumb, or the ring and the little finger are used to close the nostril. There are three variations, depending on the switching-over of the nostrils. In the first variation, the active nostril is switched after each inhalation. In the second variation, exhalation is through one nostril and inhalation through the other. After a few cycles, the inhaling and the exhaling nostrils are reversed. The third variation switches nostrils after several breaths.

This practice has three levels:

• Beginners should attempt to make the duration of inhalation and exhalation equal, and do only about six cycles of breathing. One cycle of this special breathing technique consists of one breath (inhalation and exhalation) from each nostril, or a total of two breaths.

• With practice, the duration of exhalation is slowly extended to twice the duration of inhalation, and the practice is continued for several minutes. The mind is focused on slow, deep breathing, in a manner similar to meditation.

• The advanced practice continues for ten to twenty minutes or longer, with the breath held after inhalation and/or exhalation. One is eligible to attempt this voluntary breath-holding only after being able to get a 10:20 second ratio between the inhalations and the exhalations with comfort and ease over an extended period of time.

Technique of Alternate-Nostril Breathing

• Adopt a comfortable seated posture and rest the left hand comfortably in the lap.

• With the right hand make a gentle fist and release the thumb, the little finger and the ring finger. This hand position is called the Nasika Mudra. If this position is uncomfortable you can use the thumb and the index finger.

• To start with, exhale completely. Allow the thumb to gently press the right nostril shut while the left nostril is open. Inhale slowly through the left nostril.

• Gently close the left nostril with the ring finger and exhale through the right nostril.

• Inhale through the right nostril and then close the right nostril. Exhale through the left nostril.

• Continue this pattern (exhale-inhale-switch-exhale-inhale-switch), switching from one nostril to the other, for the exhale-inhale sequence. Continue practice up to three minutes initially. With time, you can increase the duration as your stamina and endurance increase.

• During the practice, do not bend the head forward, nor apply too much pressure on the nostrils so as to bend the nose to one side.

• End the practice with an exhalation through the right nostril.

• Allow the hands to rest on the lap and sit still with eyes closed. Observe how calm and still the breath and the mind have become.

Regulating the Count

After getting comfortable with the pattern of alternate-nostril breathing, we can begin to regulate the timing, and bring balance to both nostrils.

• Begin by counting mentally, or timing the duration with the ticking of a wall clock. Each individual differs in the count and in the duration it takes to complete one cycle.

• Use the lowest count for the breath. For example, let us allocate three counts to each cycle. Exhale three, inhale three, and switch.

• Continue to increase the duration. It may vary each day. It is advisable to begin each day afresh. Do not attempt to begin from where you left off the previous day. Be slow and gentle in expanding the count. Instead of setting up a scenario for failure, set up one for comfort and ease, and you might find that the closed nostril automatically opens.

• When you are comfortable with a count of five exhalations and five inhalations, increase the length of the exhalations. Start with 4:5 then go on to 4:6 and so on till the exhalation is twice as long as the inhalation.

• Savour the breath by letting it out more slowly. Starting the exhalation with a blast produces stress. We are exhausted by the blast and cannot increase the duration of the exhalation. On the other hand, if we start slowly, we can prolong the out-breath and enjoy a rewarding experience. As we gain control, it takes longer to breathe out completely.

• With time, practice and patience, it will be possible to attain ratios of 5:10 or 6:12, and even 7:14, 8:16 and 10:20.

The test of progress is the comfort you feel at the end of practice. With ratios of 5:10 we take just four breaths per minute and there is no breathlessness, dizziness or discomfort. The body learns to economize and utilize the exchange better, and the mind too, feels more in tune with the process.

Why is it necessary to slow the breaths?

The benefits of slow, pranayamic breathing were conceptualized by yogis by observing nature. They noticed that animals that breathe slowly and steadily, like the tortoise and the elephant, live longer as compared to animals who breathe fast and spasmodically like the lion and the dog. Don't we too, readily accept that our breaths are individually metered, and that we live only as long as the desired number of breaths. So, if we can breathe more slowly, we shall have more time to complete the count of our breaths.

At the biological level too, slow breathing has been found to promote physiological balance and health with a deeper yet rejuvenating rest to the mind.

Why do we need double the time for exhalation?

Prolonged exhalation in alternate-nostril breathing and other yogic slow-breathing techniques promotes calmness and parasympathetic dominance. The slowing of the heart rate during exhalation is the result of greater parasympathetic activity during exhalation. Likewise, the increased alpha and theta brain wave activity on the EEG (electro-encephalography) reported during exhalation further brings inner balance and poise with awareness and alertness.

Benefits of Alternate-nostril Breathing

• Equalizing the breath balances the Sympathetic and the Parasympathetic Nervous Systems. This allows us to feel peaceful and balanced.

• Longer exhalations allow the PNS to get an upper hand over the SNS (usually it is the reverse). This helps break the vicious cycle of stress and disease. We give more time to the healing mechanisms in the body to take over, thus helping alleviate our physical and emotional problems.

• Induces calmness, and lowers anxiety and stress.

• Benefits respiratory disorders such as nasal allergy,

bronchitis, and asthma. It not only cleanses the nasal tract, but also provides better gas exchange and lung function.

• Reduces elevated blood pressure, acidity and other effects of high stress.

• Increases vitality as we have more life force, prana. When the nadis are purified, we have lightness of the body, radiance of complexion, better digestion, leanness, and a calm mind.

• The practice promotes a balance between the functions of the brain by optimizing the two cerebral hemispheres of the two sides of the brain.

Alternate-nostril Breathing for Balanced and All-round Development

The Brain – Subjective and Objective

The right nostril, governed by the SNS, corresponds with the functions of the left side of the brain, and its attributes of logic, reason, intellect and reason. The left nostril, governed by the PNS, corresponds with the right side of the brain, and its attributes of coolness, intuition, emotions, peace and awareness.

Our lifestyle and the education system we follow train us to use more of the left brain and ignore the faculties of the right half. We like to believe that everything in our life is rational, objective and logical (left-brain attributes), while totally ignoring the inner-directed, intuitive and creative side of our personality (right-brain functions). Science may make tall claims about its discoveries, but cannot ignore the fact that all discoveries have come initially as a flash of intuition from the right brain. Subsequently, the scientist uses his or her left brain to prove it. Albert Einstein was once asked how he had come up with the revolutionizing concept about the relationship between energy and matter. He answered in very simple words, 'I meditated and it revealed itself to me.'

The left brain is for 'thinking' and the right for 'experiencing'. The quality of consciousness in life is determined by how well they are programmed via knowledge and experience. Their relationship determines how we view and experience present the moment and plan the future. If they work in harmony, then the result is 'health'. If they are not willing to recognize each other's views, believing themselves to be independent, they generate 'dis-ease'. Like a divorced couple, the result is a fragmented mind.

Alternate-nostril breathing consists of a balance between our rational and logical, and our intuitive and creative selves to attain a mind that is comprehensive, comparative and intuitive, and that can be used to assess itself, its thoughts and emotions. The breathing serves as a technique for 'inner bonding.'

Research reconfirms that alternate-nostril breathing balances the functioning of the left and the right brain hemispheres by improving spatial orientation and spatial memory (right brain-left nostril), and also verbal expression and cognition (left brain-right nostril).

Dr. David Shannahoff-Khalsa, Director of The Research Group for Mind-Body Dynamics at the Institute for Non-linear Science at UC, San Diego, has spent twenty-five years conducting research on the nasal cycle and cerebral dominance in health and disease. According to him, 'The two hemispheres of the brain alternate in dominance naturally. That's why our moods, mental performance, drives, desires, sleep patterns, and even the severity of mental disorders change over time.'

The Heart

Research has documented the ultradian rhythms of cardiovascular activities as well – right-nostril breathing increases the heart rate and the blood pressure, while left-nostril breathing lowers them. Even the metabolism, as measured by the oxygen consumption of the body, was found to increase with right-nostril breathing as compared to the left.

In studies on patients with ischemic heart disease it has been discovered that chest pain – angina pectoris – and related stress are greatly relieved by alternate-nostril breathing. It has also been documented that the practice of alternate-nostril breathing on a regular basis is an effective means to obtain the benefits of slow, deep, diaphragmatic breathing, including parasympathetic stimulation and balanced metabolism for reducing chest pain, and decreasing the dose and the frequency of medication.

Alternate-nostril breathing can also help prevent heart disease. With the help of alternate-nostril breathing it is possible to lower the heartbeat. When we lower the frequency of the heartbeat we allow our heart to rest a little longer than usual between two consecutive contractions. This additional rest allows the heart to get filled with larger quantities of blood, and to contract with greater strength, thereby strengthening the heart muscle and maintaining it in better condition.

18

Vibrations for Healing – Ujjayi, Bhramari, and OM Chanting

To stop your mind does not mean to stop the activities of the mind. It means your mind pervades your whole body.

—Shunryo Suzuki

Building awareness and reaching the depth with vibrations and chanting

The smallest unit of matter is considered to be the atom with its subatomic particles. All forms of matter continuously emit energy. Every form has its own resonance or radiance, which exerts an effect or pressure on the surroundings. The characteristic radiance of the electron and the molecules is well known and has been studied.

Every element of this universe is in a constant state of vibration. Be it matter or energy, everything vibrates. Our human senses can perceive only a fraction of this infinite range of vibrations. We are aware of just the 'sound window' that our ears can hear. There is an ocean of vibrations that we cannot perceive with our five senses, but we realize that this does affect us and our health.

Mobile phones and Internet connectivity have made the world a small place only because of the ability of nature to transmit vibrations. Somehow human health and consciousness are dependent on unheard universal vibrations in unexpected ways. When we 'tune in to nature', watching the waves in the ocean or gazing at a lush green garden, we absorb these radiations and get a good feeling. The coincidences and the synchronies of life increase when we are 'in harmony with the universe'.

In yogic practices, this growth of our awareness progresses with the help of vibrations. Techniques that are popularly used are, Ujjayi, Bhramari and Omkaar chanting. They are very effective and interesting breathing techniques too, and offer several benefits for healing, concentration and meditation. Vibrations generated through chanting are fundamental tools for altering the psyche.

Ujjayi

Ujjayi means 'the victorious one' in Sanskrit, or the one that helps gain victory over oneself. This type of pranayama helps build awareness. It is the only pranayama that can be done standing or while walking, and can be used in combination with most other types of pranayama.

Ujjayi consists of very slow (three-four breaths per minute), smooth, maximum inhalation, followed by slow, smooth, maximum exhalation. Airflow is restricted by keeping the voice box area of the larynx and glottis in the throat partially closed which results in a soft, uniform, low hissing sound, as the air rubs across the surfaces. The mind is focused on breathing, particularly on the low hissing sound.

Technique

• Sit comfortably in any posture with ease.

• Relax the facial muscles with a gentle smile. This will not only relax you but also prevent you from overdoing the practice to a strenuous degree.

• Bring your awareness to your throat. Visualize breathing through a tiny hole in front of the throat. This way, we will partially tighten the larynx and the air will pass slowly through the throat, producing the hissing sound.

• The sound should have a low and uniform pitch and should

be pleasant to hear. It should not be audible to others but only to oneself.

• Friction of air in the nose should be avoided so that no nasal sound is heard.

• Initially, do Ujjayi only while exhaling, and then during both inhalation and exhalation.

• The Hatha Yogic texts emphasize exhalation through the left nostril. The time occupied with exhalation should be about twice as long as that of inhalation.

• Either way, after completely exhaling through the left, or both nostrils, the breath stops automatically before inhalation. Relax and enjoy this Kewal Kumbhaka as long as it is comfortably possible.

• This constitutes one round of Ujjayi. A minimum of nine rounds is recommended.

• Advanced practitioners of yoga include breath-holding after inhalation and sometimes after exhalation.

Benefits

• Ujjayi strengthens the epiglottis muscles, thus helping to reduce snoring.

• Improves the voice and helps it to become melodious, enables it to modulate the pitch with ease.

• Reduces tonsillitis, colds and sore throat, asthma, excessive hiccups and a hypersensitive throat.

• Reduces anxiety, calming the mind.

• Improves awareness.

Ujjayi – towards Meditation

One can delve deeper into the subtler plane during Ujjayi by coordinating the breaths and the hissing sound with the mental chant of a mantra such as 'So Hum' or 'Om Om': 'So' during inhalation and 'Hum; during exhalation, or one 'Om' with each phase of breathing. The hissing sound guides the mental chant, thereby producing a tranquil and balanced state of mind.

The Science behind Ujjayi Breathing

Ujjayi breathing is a slowed-down, somewhat controlled, inspiration and expiration against airway resistance. People experience a feeling of calmness on practising this form of pranayama as evidenced by the alpha activity generated on a person's EEG during Ujjayi pranayama. This indicates a shift to parasympathetic dominance—the balancing, easing and releasing mechanisms of the body. The hissing sound produced has a positive impact on the vagus nerve, which is the chief 'cable' of the rejuvenating Parasympathetic Nervous System: it works to inhibit an activated physiology and to restore energy reserves. Ujjayi is also found to enhance cerebral perfusion or increased blood flow in the brain that is necessary for very active mental processing.

CHANTING

Bhramari Chanting

The word '*bhramari*' is Sanskrit for 'female bee'. In Bhramari pranayama, a humming sound is generated during a slow exhalation, resembling the sound produced by a female bee. Ancient yogis did this pranayama for long durations to experience an ecstatic state of mind. The Bhramari, or 'humming bee' pranayama, is now recommended after a major operation to speed up healing. In reality, since it works at the deepest level where only vibrations can reach, it should be done by one and all. The vibrations help to lull the practitioner into a state of relaxation and deep healing.

Technique

• Sit with the spine erect and hands comfortably placed on the lap. Consciously relax the body with autosuggestion and wear a beautiful smile on the face.

• Ensure that the lips are closed, the rows of teeth are

separated, and the tongue is relaxed just behind the lower set of teeth. One can lightly touch the tip of the tongue to the roof of the mouth—Khechari Mudra.

• Take a deep breath and, exhaling slowly, make a low-pitched humming sound (nnnnn........ ....) like that of a bee.

• Feel the humming sound behind the soft palate and within the head.

• Promote the effortless stoppage of breath—Kewal Kumbhaka. With practice, the length of this pause increases, marking progress.

• During the Kewal Kumbhaka (pause) that follows once the humming has stopped, the vibrations resonate throughout the body. Enjoy the bliss of the pause. The joy that the practitioner gets during the Kumbhaka is unlimited and indescribable!

• Allow the inhalation to start spontaneously. Inhale deeply and repeat the sequence.

• Sit still and enjoy the sense that all is well with the world.

• In the beginning, five–ten rounds of Bhramari are enough. Slowly the practice can be increased to five or ten minutes.

Vibration and Resonance – the Crux of Chanting

Resonance is a phenomenon where the matching of frequencies from two sources produces waves of higher amplitude as the waves complement each other. The tuning of a stringed musical instrument is an example of resonance: proper tuning of the strings produces beautiful sound in every part of the instrument.

A similar fine-tuning has to be done during the practice of Bhramari. Humming should be done five times, each at a different pitch, while observing which sound vibrates the most in the body, particularly the head region. When the frequency of the sound produced matches the natural frequency of the body, one can feel the vibrations all through the body. Many people try to prolong the sound and miss the resonance that is most important in Bhramari. It is the soothing lulling effect of the resonance that merges the body and the mind into a harmonious melody.

Sound, Vibrations and Health

Experiments have provided convincing evidence that music and sound can have an effect on healing. It is found that chanting produces more T cells (chief cells of the immune system) in the saliva, indicating stronger immune systems that can withstand stress better.

Physicians like Tsunoda in 1985 showed that certain sounds lateralize to either the left or the right brain hemisphere. Bhramari and other yogic chanting techniques bring the technology of 'sound medicine' into our domain, and people in growing numbers now practise them. The subtle effects, however, can be felt only through personal experience.

The mechanism hypothesized by some scientists is that, during chanting, the tongue interacts with the upper palate (roof of the mouth) through the contact of its tip and broader surface in a very discrete and special way. The hard palate has sound-and-vibration sensitive points that get stimulated as the tongue touches them – the way our fingers interact with the keyboard of a piano. The sequential and repetitive stimulation of these points transmits effects to the higher brain centres through the thalamus and the hypothalamus.

Anatomically, the hypothalamus lies in close proximity to the palate bone. The resonance gets transmitted through the sensitive points on the palate and this affects the regional metabolism of the hypothalamus. Different sounds affect different parts of the hypothalamus. By now we know how important and strategic the hypothalamus is – that is where psychology gets to meet physiology! By harmonizing the hypothalamic functions the entire body-mind complex is benefited.

Beyond Sound ...

The yogis of ancient India knew that music plays a vital role in health. Chanting generates vibrations, and the unheard sound of the universe, the *naad*, can be felt through the resonance generated after the chant is over. It cannot be heard through the ears but by the tuning and the interaction of a person's electromagnetic field with the electromagnetic field of the cosmos.

What if I feel breathless and need to inhale immediately after the chant is over?

This means you are over-humming! You will also miss the blissful experience of the spontaneous pause, the Kewal Kumbhaka. In yogic practice there is no competition with anyone. The practice is for our own benefit. The solution is to under-chant slightly, and enjoy the resonance and the Kewal Kumbhaka that will follow.

Do I need to adopt any special pose with my hands?

Some schools of pranayama emphasize a *mudra* (pose) to internalize the sounds and make the practice more effective. Place the thumbs on the flaps of the ears, pressing them back. Lightly place the index finger on the closed eyelids to ward off any external light. Place the middle finger on the side of the nose, allowing it to remain open, and rest the fourth and the fifth fingers on the upper and lower lips. Point the elbow outward away from the head. This mudra parodies the three monkeys who embody the three principles – see no evil, speak no evil, hear no evil. This pose helps to internalize the vibrations and their effects. However, if your arms start hurting, you will get distracted by the discomfort and you may miss the vibrations and the resonance generated. Alternately, sit comfortably on the floor and place the hands on the lap, palm on palm or interlocked.

Benefits

- It sensitizes the body and the body systems to healing.

• Has a very soothing effect on the nervous system, promoting a feeling of inner balance and harmony.

• Cultivates the voice and improves it by increasing the pitch and the melody.

• Helps to reduce stress and tension, thereby reducing blood pressure, sleeplessness, anger and anxiety.

• Helps to strengthen the throat and the tonsils by improving circulation and eliminating throat ailments.

• Has a massaging and balancing effect on the thyroid gland.

• Speeds up healing of tissues all over the body, and is a good practice after any surgery.

• Improves memory and concentration, and induces a meditative state.

OM Chanting

'OM' is the symbol or the verbal expression of creation. It is present in all expressions of various faiths, wherever the power behind creation and its sustenance have to be depicted.

The syllable OM is not specific to Indian culture. It has religious significance in other religions, too. Although OM is not given any specific definition, it is considered to be a cosmic sound, a primordial sound, the totality of all sounds. The word 'Amen' used among Christians too, is said to derive from the syllable OM. It means 'May it be so'. In Arabic, a similar term 'Amin' has religious significance.

Om is also used to signify divinity and authority. In the English language the syllable 'om' occurs in words such as, omniscience meaning infinite knowledge, omnipotent meaning one with infinite powers, and omnivorous meaning eating everything. This syllable also occurs in words such as omen, which means a sign of something that is to occur in future, or ombudsman meaning a person having the authority to pronounce a verdict.

Chanting OM generates certain vibrations that have a deep and profound effect on us. After a comfortable deep breath, one can start exhaling with the chant of 'O', slowly tapering it into 'M ...', and continuing till one can exhale comfortably. The abdominal wall goes inward gradually as one chants, expelling air from the chest.

The chant should be comfortable so that there is no distress in the form of gasping for air immediately after the chant gets over. Kulvalyanandji has suggested that after the chant, the abdomen should be allowed to relax, which will be accompanied by a small inhalation. Then one can experience the pause and the stillness without taking any breath, till the desire to take the next breath arises.

The chanting of OM can be done in three progressive ways:

1. Loud chant

2. Soft whisper

3. Mental chant

Initially, it is better to chant out loud as it helps erase our inhibitions, which are an obstacle to healing. One can then proceed to a soft whisper audible only to the self. Ultimately, as the awareness increases, one proceeds to chant in the mind. If you tend to fall asleep during a mental chant start reciting it out loud again.

By chanting OM, the mind gradually becomes tranquil and all the restlessness, worries and tensions disappear. The desire to continue the mental chant also disappears, and one feels like indulging in a state of silence. This feeling of inner silence emerges without any force to concentrate. Therefore, chanting should be done lovingly in a relaxed manner.

Alternative Method of Chanting

OM is made up of three and a half syllables – A, O, and M followed by silence ...!

We can chant OM by dividing the chant into three equal parts –

one-third for A, one- third for O and one-third for M, blending
one with the other. Simultaneously, one can feel the movement
of the vibrations from the navel to the chest, the throat, and then
to the face and head. After a chant, one gets to enjoy the abode
of bliss – silence. Then after an inhalation, one proceeds with the
next chant.

Research on Chanting

The verbal stimulation and the vibrational component of the OM
chant contribute to activation of the brain. Chanting OM
decreases the metabolism and the heart rate. These findings are
interpreted as a sign of increased mental alertness in the context
of physiological relaxation. Various studies on OM chanting have
demonstrated increased concentration, memory, receiving power
of the brain, and ultimately reduced levels of fatigue.

Sound beyond Silence

Most people speak because they find speech more tolerable than
silence. For most of us, even when the mouth is silent, the mind
is screaming, and speech offers an easy distraction from the
turmoil within. Therefore, the silence of the mind is more
important than the silence of the mouth. Silence is the calmness
of the mind that enables us to hear the guiding voice of wisdom
within.

SECTION V
TAPPING THE HEALING POTENTIALS OF THE MIND

The quality of life cannot be raised unless
we raise the texture of our thoughts and
the depth of our understanding

—*Swami Chinmayananda*

In the breath, the soul finds an opportunity to speak.

—*Danna Faulds*

19

The Power of Silencing the Mind – through the Breaths

I shut my eyes in order to see.

—Paul Gauguin

A mind too active is no mind at all.

—Theodore Roethke

Your goal is not to battle with the mind, but to witness the mind.

—Swami Muktananda

The beginning of mind-management

Beneath the ups and downs of life, beneath the restless surface of the mind, there is a profound state of calm and balance. By being able to rest for small periods in that state, we can create a stable and strong mind even in the face of stress. No wonder, deep inside, we all crave for silence as it reawakens the sense of self-control.

Silence is to the mind what sleep is to the body – nourishment and refreshment. The one quality of a blessed life is the ability to appreciate and enjoy this inner silence. Most of us actually need more silence than we get. Silence does not mean an atmosphere free of all sounds. In fact, the sound of birds singing and the rain drizzling are lovely natural sounds. It is the sirens, the radio and the TV, the screeching traffic, and the discordant ring tones of cell phones that are distracting!

True silence occurs when the mind is at rest: that is when we free ourselves of the various influences around us. But silence cannot be forced. Forcible eye closure cannot bring peace. If we can access the abode of silence with a smooth flow, without force, then we will tap a new level of creativity. We will actually deepen our understanding and see our own situation much more clearly. Often we try not to think of happenings that have given rise to an unresolved emotion that is eating us from inside. Silence will spontaneously show the way, and it can be a very humbling experience to become aware of our shortcomings. This realization itself can eradicate the root cause of our ill health from our subconscious mind.

Why it is necessary to silence the mind

The mind can be called a library of thoughts – commonly a madhouse filled with unconnected and random thoughts. If we were to sit down and pen our thoughts without any editing, there would be no logical sequence. We get 60,000 thoughts a day on an average, of which 90 per cent are 'junk' thoughts.

The mind does not like a vacuum. Thoughts flit through our mind, swinging between the past and the future, because the mind is a storehouse of memories of past experiences leading to anticipation of future possibilities. The mind also harbours our emotions coming from greed, desire, anger, fear, discontent and jealousy. There is always a background chattering going on over which we usually have no control.

Every thought that the mind generates has an accompanying biochemistry flowing in the body, that is, thoughts produce chemicals in the physical body that affect its functioning and health. With our present lifestyle, governed as it is by consumerism, the mind gets obsessed with more and more petty cravings. Unfulfilled desires then lead to frustration and irrational behaviour and stress. This eventually adds up to bad health.

Thus the mind is a very powerful instrument – it can break or make! Every thought is a vibration with force and energy behind it. If negative thoughts can damage, positive ones can restore. A thought can become a very potent healing force when it comes from a peaceful mind. Therefore we need to rein in our thoughts to prevent disturbances of the mind, and the consequent effect that the mind has on health. If we are not satisfied with any aspect of our life, the only way is to understand its maker – the mind! To be conquered, the mind has to be understood. Once the negative habits of the mind are understood, they can be consciously replaced with positive ones.

The ability to silence the mind is the key to switch off the mind, enabling us to turn it on and off as we wish. There is no vacuum in nature, nor in the mind. When it gets silenced, it gets filled up with positive energy – the vital consciousness that governs the order of the universe. When we can do that, we can experience strength, confidence, happiness and health, and use the mind in a more effective way. At this stage we become the boss of our mind.

To go beyond ego, to go beyond the mind, to go beyond its chatter – silence is the answer.

The Sound of Silence

- Inner equilibrium is a gift.

- Silence speaks when all words fail.

- Learn to build up silent energy within yourself.

- It is stillness, strength and serenity.

- It is the finest of all communications.

20

Mind the Power

In the province of the mind, what one believes to be true either is true or becomes true.

—John Lilly

Mindfulness is the energy that allows us to recognize our habit energy and prevent it from dominating us.

—Thich Nhat Hanh

To stop your mind does not mean to stop the activities of the mind. It means your mind pervades your whole body.

—Shunryo Suzuki

When the mind minds the mind, matter does not matter.

—Swami Swaroopananda

Training the mind to keep you healthy

The mind has a great influence on all bodily functions. This is a fact that science has understood and accepted. It has been found that happiness of the soul, the senses and the mind keeps us healthy. A balanced mind filled with realzation and compassion is actually an insurance against illness and disability.

To be well, it is very important to understand our way of thinking and of responding to people and situations. Various life experiences and unresolved emotional conflicts keep challenging the stress-coping mechanisms of the body. One cannot really avoid these ever- increasing stressors. How we react to these threats of modern times is crucial. The key is to adapt to the change. Stress does predispose us to illnesses, but the manner in which an individual copes with it is the crucial factor that decides whether the stress will eventually lead to imbalance and disease, or will get nullified with the right attitude and the coping mechanisms.

Mind, Emotions and Health

Our thoughts and emotions influence the nervous system and the brain. Each of our basic emotions is tied to a distinct, underlying pattern of brain activity. These patterns of brain activity are linked to the immune functions of the body. The brain patterns typical of positive emotions enhance immune activity, while those typical of negative emotions change it for the worse.

The adverse effects of negative emotions on health range from frequent infections, irritable bowel syndrome, chronic pain and migraine, to rising blood pressure, increased risk of heart disease, autoimmune disorders of joints and the thyroid gland, and cancer. On the other hand, positive emotions such as happiness, compassion, hope, optimism, trust, and a feeling of being in control, strengthen immune functions and bring in good health.

The mind is where the seeds of a majority of diseases are sown. To experience a better state of health with deeper healing, it is important to unburden oneself of feelings of frustration, anxiety, fear, insecurity, uncertainty, and suspicion, all of which constantly influence our physiological, emotional, mental and physical health.

Unfortunately, we tend to take life as it comes, and then we wonder why things keep going wrong. No real progress in life ever comes haphazardly. The difficulty is that our habits and beliefs are buried deep in the subconscious mind, and we find ourselves being drawn back repeatedly into old ways and patterns of thinking.

Our attention is diverted to the gripping power of the disease rather than to the possibility of cure, thus allowing the illness to become a habit. Subconscious habits wield a great influence, and stubborn diseases usually are deeply rooted in the subconscious mind. Uprooting them from the subconscious level can cure illness. The trick is consciously to block this negative, patterned flow of thoughts and focus on fresh ideas.

Cutting-edge science and ancient wisdom have come together to show how we all have the power to change our brains, literally, by changing our minds. Research has documented the influence of our mental states on the brainwaves – the electrical activity that grossly marks the functioning of the brain. Let us now understand the dynamics of the mind and the brain so that we can understand and reach greater depths of healing.

The Conscious and the Subconscious Mind

Our mind has two dimensions – the conscious and the subconscious. The conscious mind is the rational and reasoning mind which judges, takes decisions, and has the power to choose. It is objective in nature and learns through observation and education. It is directed externally through the five senses. It also controls all our conscious activities like walking, talking, eating, etc.

The subconscious mind functions automatically, for carrying out the vital functions of the body like digestion, excretion, circulation, breathing, repairing, etc. It is a treasure trove of infinite potentials – power, memory, wisdom and health. Whether it is inventions and discoveries of modern science or masterpieces of creativity and art, the source of it all is the subconscious mind. The negative mindset that is filled with fears, anxieties, jealousy, worries and tensions, suppresses our hidden potential, our ideas, and creative thoughts. With an open, joyful and receptive attitude it is possible to access them.

The innate potential of the subconscious mind opens up when

our mindset and thoughts nurture peace, righteous action, understanding, goodwill and harmony. Doubts and worries close the doors to this source of power and healing.

Let us acknowledge that negative feelings arise from the conscious mind. Only when the conscious mind is free from negativity, will the true qualities of the subconscious mind respond. That is why it is called the subconscious mind – one that is subject to the conscious.

The subconscious mind is very receptive to suggestions from the conscious mind and follows them unquestioningly. It does not reason or rationalize or question; it just obeys the conscious mind. If we persistently carry a negative belief in the conscious domain, like 'I am very sick and cannot be healthy', the subconscious mind takes it as true. Then life continues with worsening sickness, complications and miseries. It does not occur to us that we ourselves are contributing to this situation with our negative and denying beliefs. The subconscious expresses whatever is impressed upon it.

Once the subconscious mind registers an idea or a thought, it recruits all the forces to execute it, whether it is a thought harbouring disease or the other extreme – vibrant health. So it is important to train ourselves to habitually think constructive and harmonious thoughts so that we can experience health and prosperity in all fields. Even if setbacks occur, we can handle them with a positive attitude. Emotional health is the key to success in any field.

The Subconscious Mind

It is said that by changing the mind, 'disease' can be changed to 'ease'. It is the subconscious mind that heals. Healing the subconscious too, is an art, and it aims at wholeness, integration and connection, the bringing about of a balance of body, mind and emotions.

Laws of Healing

• The instinct of self-preservation is the first law of nature, and it is the prime function of the subconscious mind.

• There is no discord or sickness where the conscious and the subconscious minds are working in harmony.

• The natural tendency of the subconscious mind is to create harmony and equilibrium, unless it is poisoned by the negative thoughts and beliefs of the conscious mind, such as anger, hatred, fear and mistrust, which cause disease.

• The innate powers and the intelligence of the subconscious mind can heal when opened with life-giving constructive thoughts of faith, wholeness, beauty and understanding.

• Healing or wholeness is a result of a positive mental attitude, of thinking with faith.

• Speaking to the subconscious mind with faith, authority and conviction improves its response to our thoughts.

Can we isolate the subconscious mind functionally? And if so, can we really communicate with our subconscious mind?

Yes, we can! To satisfy our logical mind to accept these laws of healing, we need to understand the conscious and the subconscious mind in terms of measurable forms such as brainwave activity.

Brainwave Activity

The brain is made up of millions of nerve cells or neurons, each of which has its own function and duty to perform. The brain receives messages from the outside world via the sensory organs, as well as from the internal organs of the body and the muscles. The brain then decides how we must act and how we must not, according to our previously recorded experiences and memory. The brain directs all the various systems of the body and the activities that it performs. The brain cells communicate with each other through electrical impulses transmitted along a very intricate network of nerve fibres.

As we can see, the brain is a complex computer which produces electrical activity that is measured as brainwaves. These brainwaves are fine electrical movements that can be measured using the electroencephalogram (EEG). Electrodes placed on the scalp measure their frequency in cycles per second, or Hertz. From the highest to the lowest frequency, these brainwaves are called beta, alpha, theta and delta. By studying their pattern, one can get an idea of the level of consciousness on which the brain is functioning. The following table explains the four different brainwave states:

Brainwaves	State of Consciousness	Frequency
Beta brainwaves	Waking conscious state, alert	14-30 Hz
Alpha brainwaves	Daydreaming, creative, relaxed, closed-eyed	8-13 Hz
Theta brainwaves	Dreaming, hypnotic, meditative, subconscious, athletic 'in the zone'	4-7 Hz
Delta brainwaves	Unconscious, asleep, fast asleep	0.5-6 Hz

The theta state is where much of our subconscious potential lies and where the subconscious mind is totally dominant.

Beta state—this is the normal, wakeful and thinking state of mind. At this time, the brainwaves have a frequency of 14-30 Hz or cycles per second. In beta, the mind is focused externally to receive and process information as an individual listens, thinks, applies logic, analyses and makes decisions. Beta helps us to function consciously in the world when we work, drive, go to school, etc.

Alpha state—this state reflects a relaxed yet wakeful mind with a brainwave frequency of 8-13 Hz. The individual is fully aware but in a more receptive state of mind than in beta. When we rest (not sleep), daydream, become calm or when we meditate, our brainwaves are in alpha. This state is more stable when the eyes are closed. When we engage in creative endeavours such as imagining or visualizing, our brainwaves register in alpha. The alpha state enables us to remember our dreams, which occur in the next state – the theta.

Theta state—this state occurs between wakefulness and sleep, and has a slower rate of brainwaves, 4-7 Hz. When asleep and dreaming, the brain registers a predominant theta wave form. When awake and aware, memories, eluded thoughts and answers to our problems seem to appear in theta, out of the blues! Thus, theta wave has also been identified as the 'gateway' to learning, creativity, insight and superb memory. It has been reported that just a 5-15 minutes' rest in the theta state can reduce mental fatigue. One is in theta during deep meditation, too.

Delta state—these waves make up the unconscious mind and exist in deep sleep, when the wave frequency ranges from 0.5-6 Hz. At the slowest delta frequency, the sleep is deep and dreamless. Delta is also the state where the damaged cells recover and get healed. Research has shown that, during delta, a larger number of human growth hormones is released, and damaged cells get healed more quickly.

After an extended period in the beta state, the ratio between potassium and sodium goes out of balance, resulting in mental fatigue. In the delta state, the brain cells reset this sodium and potassium ratio. We are all aware that rest and good sleep help us recover faster from injuries and fatigue.

Any state of mind is a combination of these waves, with predominance of a pattern – the beta wave frequency is related to the active functioning of the brain; the alpha rhythm is related to the receptive state of the brain; the theta rhythm is related to the concentrated one-pointed frame of mind; the delta rhythm occurs almost exclusively during deep sleep. As the brainwave patterns transit from beta to alpha to theta to delta, there is better synchronization in the human brain, which means that the entire brain is in complete harmony. This is accompanied by a satisfying rest, creative insight, moments of genius, and faster healing.

During the course of the day, the brainwaves keep moving through all the four stages. The brain can function simultaneously in more than one brainwave state. For example, we can be in beta as we enter alpha. We may be completely awake one moment and then feel more relaxed by shutting our eyes, all in a few seconds. We could also be dreaming (theta) and come up into wakefulness (beta) and then go back into a higher frequency of theta than before.

The Conscious vs. the Subconscious Mind and the Brainwaves

The mind, both conscious and subconscious, has direct influence on the brain's activity, and this can be seen in the form of brainwaves. When the conscious mind directs the activity of the brain, the beta rhythm predominates, reflecting in a state of mental activity and alertness. Too high a beta frequency can make one feel stressed out, anxious and breathless.

As for the subconscious mind, it becomes dominant as the brainwave slows through alpha to theta towards delta. When the subconscious mind directs the activity of the brain, then the alpha and the theta rhythms predominate, reflecting a state of concentration, one-pointed perception, awareness and introversion. Slowing down of the brainwaves generates greater clarity, sharpness and flexibility of the mindset than in a normal state of mind.

Alpha is the transition – the bridge – between our conscious and subconscious mind. That is when both the functional aspects of the mind, the conscious and the subconscious, can work in harmony, in an optimum state.

Alpha State – a Bridge to the Potential of the Subconscious Mind

Being in alpha is like standing at an open door with the conscious mind on one side and the subconscious mind on the other. We are conscious and, at the same time, we have an access to our subconscious mind. It is the best time to reprogramme our subconscious mind. This is why we always have our light-bulb moment when we are in alpha brainwaves.

Often, when we wake up, we can still recall our dream, just for a few short moments. That is when we are in alpha. The moment we are fully awake, we forget the dream because we are then in the beta state.

Every self-improvement course stresses that the best time to do our affirmation or visualization (techniques used to reprogramme our subconscious mind) is before we sleep and after we wake up, when we are in the alpha state. In that state, our conscious mind is less dominant, and our subconscious mind is coming to the forefront. Since the subconscious mind does not register the difference between imaginary reality and physical reality, but merely does what it is told or shown, autosuggestions can have a powerful effect in that state.

The alpha state is also considered by many as the 'gateway' to a state of creativity and genius. It is the 'optimum state of mind', where, with a relaxed and calm mind, one can access the wealth of creativity and inspiration that lies just below the conscious awareness, simultaneously processing information in a balanced perspective. And this is where we can tap the healing potentials of the subconscious mind.

The Optimum State of Mind

In the normal waking state, we react automatically to what we experience around us. Our habitual picture of the environment dominates, and we expect that everything will remain the way we already know it. When we are in a relaxed state, we no longer react automatically to thoughts and impressions. Haven't we experienced a light-bulb moment when we are bathing and a sudden idea sparks the mind, or when we suddenly get the solution to a problem just before sleeping?

If we observe carefully, we will realise that creative ideas always come to us when we are relaxed. We can then observe everything with fresh eyes and see through the filters through which life is normally experienced. We could call this a 'third-person attitude'. The mind becomes more creative and flexible: we find it easier to see things from a new perspective. We communicate more clearly and cooperate better with others. This state of the mind can be called the 'optimum state'.

Brainwave Pattern during the Optimum State of Mind

The most prominent component of the EEG is a fairly regular pattern of characteristically synchronized alpha rhythms in an adult human being who is at rest, with the body totally free of stress, and functioning in a state of profound metabolic balance corresponding to its peak capacity, allowing the mind to wander freely.

Some scientists believe that genius is not through the genes but that it is the result of the brain having been nurtured and trained to work in the alpha and the theta stages, opening up the potential of the subconscious mind. The relationship between our brainwaves and the state of consciousness can be simplified thus:

The conscious mind   Beta wave

The gateway   Alpha wave

The subconscious mind   Theta wave

The unconscious mind   Delta wave

When we are in beta, we are in the conscious realm and have no access to the subconscious mind. When we are in theta, we are in the subconscious realm with no access to the conscious dimension. That is why most people cannot remember exactly what they had dreamt about. When alpha is missing, the link with the subconscious mind is broken.

Thus the brainwave pattern during the optimum state is a combination of waves in the correct proportion and relationship with each other: the intuitive, creative awareness and insight of theta, the relaxed, detached yet bridging state of alpha, and the ability to consciously process and comprehend thoughts with the help of beta waves. In that state, man has the ability to think, act, and discriminate optimally, and all the mental capacities coordinate perfectly with each other.

Scientists usually associate this state with creativity and the 'spark of genius'. People who can tap into this state are able to access the wealth of creativity that lies just below the conscious awareness. Many geniuses can engage in that state, the most remarkable example is that of Albert Einstein who took afternoon naps and frequent periods of rest while he was working. Scientists believed that he was tapping into this 'spark of genius' state.

So, by controlling our brainwaves, we can control our state of mind. By accelerating or slowing our brainwaves, we can alter how we think, feel and act. We will feel more in charge of our emotions and our responses to the world because we will be more cognizant of the difference between reality and fleeting emotions. The result wll be clarity of thought and mind, creativity, stress management, emotional and physical well-being, and self-healing.

The Optimum Mind for Healing and Health

The brainwave state that would be ideal for healing would be an appropriate combination of theta, alpha and beta waves. Why?

First, theta waves would allow us to tap the potential of the subconscious mind, the deeper resources, and the obedient mind where we can install effective input. They would provide the depth – the subconscious inner space – where the self-healing gets programmed in the body.

Secondly, alpha waves would provide the connection, the bridge between the subconscious and the conscious mind so that the flow of information for healing could be maintained. Alpha waves would, therefore, produce a sharper and clearer form of imagery and communication. This would also enable us to remember the contents of the theta. If one were to reach theta without the alpha, one would not remember the meditation.

Lastly, beta brainwaves would allow us consciously to feed

positive images, to communicate thoughts, ideas and needs to the subconscious mind, and also to understand feelings, experiences and solutions at the conscious level.

Eureka!

This fundamental paradigm shift transforms our understanding of the human mind and also our approach to health and healing. It is possible to reset our happiness meter, regain the use of limbs disabled by stroke, train the mind to break cycles of depression, reverse age-related changes in the brain, and many more previously unimaginable feats for better health.

We can tap the healing potential of the subconscious mind for better health if we proceed as follows:

• **Mental housekeeping** – to release the burden of unresolved negative emotions from the mind

• **Connect with the subconscious mind consciously** – to attain the optimum state where we can guide the subconscious mind for better health.

• **Self programming** – communicating with the subconscious mind for better health and healing

As the excitement increases, let us proceed further on our journey.

21

Mental Housekeeping

The life that is not examined is not worth living.

—Plato

Healing is about letting go of everything that isn't you – all your expectations, all of the beliefs – and becoming who you are.

—Rachel Remen

The human mind is the last great unexplored continent on earth.

—Earl Nightingale

Inward communication is a need, not a luxury.

It has been rightly said that the quality of our relationships often has much more to do with how often we get sick and how soon we get well, rather than with genes, diet and other factors.

We all long for freedom from disease and other suffering. Most of us tend to focus our attention on the cure of bodily problems because they are so obvious. We do not realize that mental disturbances such as worry and egoism are the real cause of misery and disease. To prevent disease, one has not only to exercise and eat right, but also to get rid of the mental bacteria of anger, fear, consciousness of failure, lack of initiative and purpose, scepticism, a doubting mentality, and a solely materialistic outlook in life.

Mental hygiene – keeping the mind pure – is superior to physical hygiene, but we cannot, of course, totally ignore the latter! Instead of becoming blind to the laws of life and also to our own divinity and powers, we should cultivate a healthy attitude of mind.

It is time we realized that we are missing something in life. Learning the art of living is not just acquiring possessions and knowledge – it goes far beyond that. We need to:

• make the heart stronger by making it more open for experiencing love;

• balance the mind with the heart by allowing decisions from the head to pass through the heart;

• learn the skills of action so that it becomes enjoyable but not binding;

• start trusting the forces of life that have sustained us till date and will continue to do so;

• become sensitive to the needs of the people around us;

• practise forgiving from the heart.

Catch the Mouse – Identifying the Root Cause of Ill Health

Medical research continues to reveal, more and more, how our mind plays a powerful role in ill health and disease. Our beliefs and ways of interpreting and responding to stressors in life determine the outcome. The degree to which we feel limited and trapped by them depends on what meaning we give to a particular experience. This decides the significance of events. One person may consider loss in business as a sign of failure, while another views it as a challenge to start out afresh and improve. What meaning we attach to events depends on our belief system.

To be free of limited beliefs that create negative meanings which, in turn, lead to a blockage in the flow of life energy and to a vicious cycle of misery and ill health, one has to explore alternative interpretations and ways of responding. For that, we have to break through our limited thinking and experience life differently.

In order to break the bondage of our habits and beliefs when responding to stress, we must first identify the stressors in life. It has been observed that the stressors giving rise to disease are usually 'raw', or have occurred six months to a year and a half earlier.

How To Identify Triggering Events

The first step in trying to get well is to identify the stressors, and our personal attitudes, beliefs and behaviour towards them, which are making us sick and hopeless. The objective behind these exercises is to not relive the stress, or 'to blame' ourselves or someone else, for having been the contributing factor, but rather to identify our **beliefs and behaviour that we now want to change**.

As it is the associated attitudes that threaten our health, it is necessary to examine them to alter decisively our way of responding to them. By acknowledging the tensions that predispose us to illness, it is possible to eliminate their effects. Mere external suppression at the cost of internal tussle and disease is not worthwhile. There are three 'protocols' suggested to make the job easier. If one does not work, the next one may be the right one for us.

1.Events as stressors

Dr. Thomas Holmes and Dr. Rahe of the Washington School of Medicine have designed a scale that gives a numerical value to common stressors. One identifies the stressors, adding the corresponding values to get a rough estimate of the overall stress that one is going through at that moment. The stressors have to be identified if they have occurred in the last one to one and a half years. Beyond that, our body adjusts, and usually they are no longer a reason to get worried about.

The way we respond to stress determines their course and effect on us, which the scale cannot determine accurately since the response varies from individual to individual. We can, however, use the same list just to identify the possible reasons leading to stress, and eventually work upon them.

Social Re-adjustment Rating Scale by Dr. Holmes and Dr. Rahe

Event	Value
Death of spouse	100
Divorce	73
Marital separation	65
Jail term	63
Death of close family member	63
Personal injury or illness	53
Marriage	50
Fired from work	47
Marital reconciliation	45
Retirement	45
Change in family member's health	44
Pregnancy	40
Sex difficulties	39
Addition to family	39
Business readjustment	39
Change in financial status	38
Death of a close friend	37
Change to a different line of work	36
Change in number of arguments with spouse	35
Loan or mortgage	31
Foreclosure of mortgage	30

Event	Value
Change in responsibilities at work	29
Son or daughter leaving home	29
Trouble with in-laws	29
Outstanding personal achievement	28
Spouse begins or stops work	26
Starting or finishing school	26
Change in living conditions	25
Change in personal habits	24
Trouble with boss	23
Change in work hours, conditions	20
Change of residence	20
Change of school	20
Change of recreation	29
Change in religious activities	19
Change in social activities	18
Loan or mortgage (minor)	17
Change in sleeping habits	16
Change in number of family get-togethers	15
Change in eating habits	15
Vacation	13
Major festival	12
Minor violations of the law	11

TOTAL:

Results (assessed over the previous twelve months):

More than 300 points: Such people are more prone to all kinds of illnesses and need more energy to stay healthy.

200-299 points: This level too, indicates an above-average stress level and makes the person prone to illnesses.

100-199 points: The risk of ill health is low.

Having gone through the list, all these experiences of life seem common, but what varies is the reaction of an individual to them, and that is what determines emotional health. Our self-conversation – the internal dialogue we have with our mind – determines our attitude. For example, we may be focused on fighting a disease, but if our core belief is that it is an incurable disease, our brain will go into overdrive, processing the negative self-conversation in such a manner that it hampers healing. Allowing our negative beliefs to rule our interior prevents us from becoming healthy and happy; such beliefs paralyse us and lead to unresolved emotions.

1. Identifying Unresolved Emotions and Beliefs

Our mind runs at high speed, day and night! We are plagued with sad and tormenting thoughts. When there is too much annoyance bottled up, it turns into poison. Then, we are conditioned to consider some emotions as bad and we unknowingly programme ourselves not to be aware of them. We cover them up with countless thoughts to insulate ourselves from feeling and confronting what needs attention. Actually negative feelings originate from a narrow-minded personal point of view, leading to unhealed wounds. Some deep wounds may be very old but still raw. Their emotional component has not yet been resolved leading to a vicious cycle of misery and disease. The network of events is so interconnected that it is difficult to frame them as a sentence in the mind. To resolve them, their identification is necessary. It has been said that fear fades as the facts are faced. The following table lists the common emotional grudges, unresolved emotions, and negative beliefs that we may be carrying:

Negative Beliefs: I am ...	Uresolved Emotions
... unworthy	Fear or worry of:
... undeserving	• disease·
... incapable	• failure, rejection·
... misunderstood	• being alone·
... abandoned	• heights, dogs, water, snakes·
... betrayed	• public speaking·
... unproductive	• injections, dentist·
... unattractive	• death
... a failure	Insecurity over ...
... a victim	Anger against ...
... a burden	Hatred of ...
... dumb	Anxiety over promotion Future
... used	of my ...
... alone	Depressed about ...
... bad	Craving for ...
... guilty	Jealousy of ...
... sinful	Guilt over ...
... confused	Rejected/Abandoned by...
... trapped	Nightmares about ...
... unlovable	Memory of ...
... powerless	Doubt against ...
... inferior	Discomfort
... vulnerable	Restlessness
... incompetent	
... betrayed	
... abused	
... stupid	

2. People as Stressors

Our thoughts and beliefs cannot be a substitute for our feelings. We usually associate our stress and its effects with the people with whom we have interacted, and with the way they have made us feel. Some make us feel good and positive, while others, whom we remember more easily, are the ones who trigger the entire event – that vicious cycle in our system – throwing us off balance. Suppression adds more fuel to the fire. It is worth our while to bravely acknowledge a bad situation, and to figure out how we responded to it so that we can change our behaviour now.

On the other hand, we take many acquaintances for granted, especially our near and dear family members. As life goes on, we meet more people and we forget about them. Many of them have contributed to our present success and happiness. This acknowledgement will help develop humility in us, and an attitude of gratitude towards them and life. This positive emotion helps in the healing process. It is not necessary to call them physically to say 'Thank you' – a mental attitude of thankfulness would suffice. At times, the incidents might be so old that offering thanks at the present moment would be a socially inappropriate act. Just acknowledging in the mind would be enough.

Introspection leads to a path of self-discovery, humility and happiness. Thus, the purpose of this analysis is to do a thorough mental housekeeping.

Sit undisturbed and at ease, and think back on all the people you have interacted with to date. Divide them into three categories:

1. People to whom we need to be thankful.

2. People to whom we need to apologize.

3. People whom we need to forgive.

	Thankful to	Apologize to	Forgive
Childhood	1. 2.	1. 2.	1. 2.
School	1. 2.	1. 2.	1. 2.
College	1. 2.	1. 2.	1. 2.
Work	1. 2.	1. 2.	1. 2.
Family	1. 2.	1. 2.	1. 2.
Friends	1. 2.	1. 2.	1. 2.
Relatives	1. 2.	1. 2.	1. 2.

Doing this exercise itself releases half the emotional burdens from the mind. Somehow, it also shows the way to handling the person or the situation.

Simplified Stepwise Approach

From time to time, our mind too, needs to be cleansed of negative thoughts; otherwise the energy paths get congested, preventing us from thinking clearly. We all desire a strong, healthy mind. Here is a stepwise approach to mental housekeeping as proposed by Carl Simonton, one of the pioneers in the field of self-healing techniques.

1. List the five major stresses in your life right now.

2. Examine the ways in which you may be participating in maintaining the stresses.

3. Consider the ways to remove them from your life.

4. If there is no way to remove the stress, consider whether you are creating other balancing and nurturing elements in your life, like accepting the support of good friends, giving yourself pleasurable experiences, expressing your feelings about the situation.

5. Consider whether you can remove these stresses or balance them in your life by putting your own needs first more often. Attempt to find ways to meet with your needs.

With all these exercises, we are now ready to accept responsibility for our health and its betterment. Self-examination unearths clues about how we can now change our self-destructive behaviour and beliefs. Just as we have contributed to the disease, we also have the power to participate in our recovery.

Once we take a decision to alter our behaviour, the body responds with hope as the mental state creates a re-enforced programme of healing and renewal. Since the mind, the body and the emotions act as one system, changes in our way of thinking influence physical health, too. The cycle of recovery continues as improvement in our physical state further injects hope and vitality. There are many examples of recoveries that could be considered as miracles. In many cases, physical and mental health improve significantly, and people start feeling 'weller than well'.

Forgiveness

It has been rightly said, 'No real healing can occur without forgiveness.' Forgiveness is for all of us. It is easier to forgive when we accept that we are responsible for the state in which we are. By deciding to forgive we actually decide to close an issue that otherwise refuses to go away. If we do not forgive, we are held back while the other person moves on. The sufferer is not the one who inflicted the pain of the event but the one who is still holding on to it.

Forgiving does not mean accepting someone's wrong act. That would be unfair! Forgiveness means deciding to let go the hurt and the pain, and regaining control of our life and emotions. It eases the burden of revenge and hatred, and allows us to move ahead in life. Consider these words – 'As long as you do not forgive, who or whatever it is, it occupies rent-free space in your mind.'

Forgiveness does not necessarily mean reconciling. By forgiving, we move on. We consciously step out of the trap and the episode that caused us pain. The burden of the past gets released as we decide not to let hatred or anger take over. By forgiving we release the burden of unresolved emotions from our nervous system. This washes us with a flow of positive energy that has been found beneficial for our health – by reducing blood pressure, relieving stress-associated pain, depression, etc.

Attitude of Gratitude and Surrender

Turning towards a force that is greater than we are is a powerful tool for unlocking our limitless potential. Turning inwards means becoming receptive and open to clues and responses, and thereby, growing in awareness of the healing forces within and around us.

High, exalted mountains are barren and lonely. Nothing nurtures them – neither rain nor crops, while forests and meadows grow in expansive open valleys. In our pride we become unapproachable and nothing seems to work. By climbing down and becoming a valley we receive the rewards of well-being and joy. Fruits can grow only when we are receptive to the seeds.

The second step is to find simple and effective ways of building up awareness, and awakening the healing powers of the subconscious mind. This awareness can be called mindfulness.

As a medical intervention, mindfulness has proven effective in helping to alleviate symptoms, facilitating healing, and helping relieve the suffering of people with chronic disease.

Healing through mindfulness involves mastering our brainwaves, and altering them from the purely waking state towards that of optimum functioning of the subconscious mind. In that state we can then do self-programming, that is, programme the software of the mind to a state of receptivity where autosuggestions can be given. This is done through techniques that make us move from worry and fear towards expectancy and faith to heal.

Tips to Everlasting Good Health

• Treat yourself like your own child in a loving and friendly way.

• Have a positive attitude – whatever happens is for the good.

• Engage in hard work that you love.

• Have a clean conscience – let your thoughts, words and actions match.

• Treat everyone better than what you think of them.

• Forgive other people and yourself.

• Practise gratitude and appreciation.

• Do not judge too much; see things as they are.

• View every experience as a gift – learn from it and go ahead.

• Raise your consciousness to acceptance rather than resistance.

• Caring is what connects us to the world, and heals us.

• Anything that leads to peace of mind takes us in the right direction.

• Take life as it comes, and enjoy the abundance of your existence at every moment.

These are golden words, repeated from time immemorial, but we need them in the present times to prevent our hectic striving for pleasure and success from consuming us. In reality, these qualities lie within us. Our clouded mind stops us from realizing them. By realizing them we actually develop our true personal nature and strength.

We do not have to suppress our negative feelings by covering them with a mask of holiness. We just have to open ourselves up and savour the deep joys of balanced living.

22

Connecting with the Subconscious Mind Consciously through Pranayama

You need all your energy for silence of the mind, and it is only in emptiness, in complete emptiness, that a new thing can be.

—J. Krishnamurti

During periods of relaxation after concentrated activity, the intuitive mind seems to take over and can produce sudden clarifying insights.

—Fritjof Capro, Physicist

Reaching the optimum state of mind

There are many cases of people who have got completely healed of incurable diseases such as cancer. There are others who feel healed and live with zeal despite the background illness and the breaking of all norms! What is it that heals them? They must definitely do something to handle their thought process, attitude, mindset and the energy dynamics of their body. Can we too, not do something more to experience a better state of health?

Yes, we can! It has been observed that there are more chances of healing when the physical techniques – medicines, exercise, and diet – are combined with the techniques of mind-management and energy enhancement.

Consciously controlling our brainwaves is the first step towards healthy living. When we control our brainwaves, we control the way we think, feel, reason and react. Relaxation, creativity and self-awareness flow naturally, and our physical health improves.

Most of us would like to function with this optimum state of mind but are not sure how to achieve that state. Some argue that it is not possible to control the state of our mind except through years of practising meditation, when the waking beta brainwaves slow down to the states of alpha and theta. While trying to work our way to experiencing this inner state, we are brought short by the mind, which gives all sorts of reasons for why it is better not to bring it under control. Nobody – including the mind – wants to be ruled by someone else!

What are the commonly known techniques, which, if practised regularly, individually or in combination, will allow us to become aware of how quiet and still the mind can be, and prepare us for a marvellous voyage to the centre of our being where the secret to health and happiness lies? The techniques for attaining this state are:

- Physical relaxation
- Meditation

Physical Relaxation

People suffering from chronic diseases believe their body has betrayed them and, unknowingly, they start hating it as if it were the enemy. This leads to a lack of faith in its self-healing capacities. Learning to relax the body helps them to accept the illness, and to develop trust in the body's ability to heal. It also reduces associated fears especially in life-threatening diseases.

For most of us, relaxation involves activities like watching television or competitive sports, or reading about the fluctuating stock market rates and the rising cost of living. This type of 'relaxation', which registers waves of excitement and alarm in the brain, actually shifts our usual thoughts to another set of thoughts which can only be termed as 'killing time', and are not, truly speaking, relaxation.

In real relaxation, with the physical softening of the body, the breathing becomes easier, and the mental chatter of thoughts settles down to a level where there is a certain degree of detachment from our problems, and where the tensions melt away. We turn off our exterior world and feel calmer than usual.

In Yoga Nidra (yogic sleep), done in Shavasana (lying supine, flat), one consciously takes the awareness to each part of the body, observing, and then letting go off, of any tightness and stress. This way, one is able to relax the body with a fully aware mind. As the muscles relax and the breathing slows down, the brainwave pattern shifts towards alpha and theta.

One very common sequel is falling asleep and that is not Yoga Nidra! If one can maintain awareness in a relaxed body, the mind has the optimum mix of alpha, theta and beta for self-healing.

Generally, it is easier to relax the body with our eyes closed because this reduces the distractions and the impulses for strong beta discharge in the brain. It is not a crime to fall asleep in this state. But if you want to go deeper into the subconscious mind with a certain degree of awareness, falling asleep will defeat the purpose.

Meditation

Meditation is a state of mind that leads to the higher states of awareness. To achieve this state one needs to still the mind, to control the thoughts, and to balance the emotions. Meditation reflects brainwaves close to the theta-alpha states while maintaining awareness and alertness.

The value of meditation in alleviating suffering and promoting healing has been known and practised for thousands of years. More and more doctors now prescribe meditation as a way of lowering blood pressure, improving exercise performance in people with angina, helping people with asthma to breathe easier, relieving insomnia, and generally relaxing the everyday stresses of life.

A wealth of research studies confirms the benefits of meditation:

it helps to reduce stress and anxiety, increase exercise tolerance, sharpen perception, increase awareness, improve concentration, maintain health, provide a general positive outlook on life, and foster the development of a sense of personal meaning in the world. Meditation is a safe and simple way to balance a person's physical, emotional, and mental states.

Regular practice of meditation helps to achieve this, but for the common man meditation is not a part of the daily routine for various reasons:

- Lack of time

- Sluggishness and sleepiness

- An itchy and distracted state of mind

- Unavailability of learning resources

- Something coming in the way – family, responsibilities, duties, hobbies

- Lack of patience – silencing the mind does not happen overnight

- Foggy and dizzy states leading to fear

- A restless and racing mind

We need to identify simple methods which are accessible to the common man, and which **require us to 'do something' to attain the optimum state of mind.** Are there techniques which are within the reach of one and all? **Yes, there are, and pranayama is the answer!**

The breathing techniques of pranayama have lots to offer in this context. They smoothly induce brainwaves towards alpha and beyond – the optimum state of mind. Reaching the optimum state through pranayama is simple and tangible. Unfortunately, we only look to the physical effects of pranayama. There is no doubt that pranayamic techniques of breathing are good for the body, and they do increase our reservoirs of energy. They also have a positive, calming and relaxing effect on the mind. But that is not the end of the story.

Management gurus teach us how to tap 'Mind Power' to create success in life. We too, can use the powers of the mind for better health, and the technique is pranayama. Owing to its positive influence on the faculties of the mind, pranayama can be used in a very tangible way to reach the deeper levels and to tap the potential of the mind for self-healing.

Pranayama and the Optimum State of the Mind

Breathing not only affirms our life, but it also affects our health and well-being at every level. Shallow, restricted and erratic breathing contributes to physical illness, emotional and mental problems. Relaxed, full, rhythmic and free-flowing breathing enhances the functions of all bodily systems, releasing tension, replenishing energy, calming the mind, and thus restoring balance. In every respect, on every level, breath is a powerful healing force.

We can access the advantages of being connected in alpha any time we want. Gaining mastery over the mind by gaining mastery over the breath is the most tangible way, and the best technique for this is pranayama. By consciously influencing the breath, one can create a very efficient therapeutic system. With pranayama, our mind registers an optimum state that is receptive and creative, and this increases endorsement in the subconscious mind. With continued practice we start going deeper and we feel a sense of increasing joy and peace. As our conscious desire for good health merges with the subconscious, it comes back reinforced with the power to influence the conscious mind and fulfil the desire.

Pranayama leads us to the path of holistic living marked by health, harmony, peace and efficiency. The *Hatha Yoga Pradipika* says:

'When the breath is irregular, the mind is unsteady, but when the breath is still, so is the mind still, and the Yogi obtains the power of stillness.'

Yoga Sutra, the well known yogic scripture by Rishi Patanjali throws light on this aspect of pranayama as well:

'Pranayama is cessation of the movement of inhalation and exhalation and thus the covering of the light is dissolved and the mind is fit for concentration.'

Each of the breathing practices discussed earlier in this book has the potential to lead us to the desired optimum state of mind where health and healing can be accessed with greater ease: Kapalabhati and Bhastrika, the pauses after the cleansing breaths; Anuloma Viloma Pranayama, the slow and rhythmic breaths of alternate-nostril breathing; Ujjayi, the victorious breaths; or the soothing hums of Bhramari and OM chanting.

Physiologically, the 'happenings' during the breathing practices that lead to the brainwave state of synchrony and optimization are:

- Pauses, Kumbhaka

- Conscious slowing done of the rate of breathing with an increase in depth (diaphragmatic breathing)

- Vibrations generated during the humming and chanting

The Pause – Silence

Each cycle of breathing is usually thought of as a single inhalation, followed by a single exhalation. The transition between the two phases is important because it involves reversals in the direction of the flow, and the movement of muscles and lungs. These pauses in the activity of breathing, when the reversal occurs, are important because they help us develop physically, emotionally and mentally.

Pauses in our breathing are the abode of bliss, knowledge, creativity and freedom. In deep meditation, during mindful pranayama, or during relaxation, the breathing can become gradually fainter and eventually stop by itself – for a while. This is described as the highest form of pranayama.

When are the pauses felt?

• With rapid breathing (Kapalabhati and Bhastrika), the breath automatically gets suspended between groups of rapid breaths for just a few seconds initially and, after more practice, for as long as is comfortable.

• With regular practice of deep yogic and alternate-nostril breathing techniques, the breaths automatically get held for a short while, especially after exhalation.

• In more advanced practice, the breaths are consciously but comfortably held after inhalation and exhalation, using techniques known as bandhas or locks. The mind is focused inward during breath-holding, and is concentrated on a particular area of the body such as the heart or the forehead regions.

We can easily experience the optimum state with cleansing breaths and the slow, deep breathing techniques of pranayama. Research documents that pranayama leads to alpha and theta wave production. How do these techniques lead to this optimum state of mind?

Optimum State with the Cleansing Breaths

The mechanisms by which cleansing breathing exercises like Bhastrika and Kapalabhati lead to a state of calm and balance are:

• The practice leads to an initial excitation of the Central Nervous System (CNS), with a subjective experience of stimulation, followed immediately by relaxation during the spontaneous pause. This leads to stimulation of the visceral (related to the internal organs in the abdominal cavity) nerve endings, which eventually activates the Parasympathetic Nervous System (calming and relaxing).

• The activation of the temporo-parietal cortical areas of the brain leads to a subjective experience of excitation during the breathing, and is followed by emotional calming with mental activation and alertness during the Kewal Kumbhaka or the pause, and the slowing down of the breaths.

In a recent study, variations in the EEG pattern were studied during various phases of pranayamic breathing, using specific parameters, namely correlation dimension (CD) and fractal dimension (FD). The values were higher for Pooraka (inhalation), lower for Rechaka (exhalation), and still lower for the Kumbhaka (pause) stage.

The reduction in the values for Kumbhaka is representative of a less complex brain process. The frequency of the EEG signal falls and hence the mind relaxes more. So, the longer the duration of the Kumbhaka stage, the greater the relaxation. This suggests that when the subject is in the Kumbhaka state, the number of active, parallel, functional processes in the brain gets reduced, and the brain goes into a more relaxed state. This gives rise to an increase in alpha frequencies in the brainwaves.

Slow, Deep, Rhythmic Breathing

Pranayamic breathing has been defined as a manipulation of the breath movement. It has been shown to contribute to a physiologic response that is characterized by the presence of decreased oxygen consumption, a decreased heart rate, and decreased blood pressure, as well as an increased alpha and theta wave amplitude in EEG recordings, and an increased parasympathetic activity accompanied by the experience of alertness and reinvigoration.

Various studies have revealed that if the deep muscles are relaxed, human subjects show more alpha activity and only a little beta activity. On the other hand, with tensed muscles there was very little alpha activity but considerable beta activity. It has been observed that the slowing of breaths decreases muscle tension toward relaxation levels, and enhances alpha activity in the brain. It has been further suggested that attention to breathing slows its rate, and hence, concentration is essential for fine-tuning awareness.

The physiological advantage of slow breathing itself generates easy and spontaneous pauses (Kumbhaka), the benefits of which have been discussed above.

Sound Vibrations and the Brain

Specific sound vibrations have been shown to influence the metabolic functions of the body, reducing anxiety and leading to mental restlessness. Research has revealed that alpha wave synchronization and intensity increase at certain sound frequencies, while the vibrations of OM induce alpha and theta activity in the brain.

Pranayama and the Optimum State of Mind

This can be achieved with:

• Kewal Kumbhaka, after Kapalabhati and Bhastrika

• The slow, deep, gentle breathing of Anuloma Viloma Pranayama, Ujjayi Pranayama

• Kumbhaka – spontaneous or induced between the phases of breathing

• Soothing vibrations of Bhramari and OM chanting

Pranayama smoothly induces the brain to reach the optimum state when the subconscious gets activated. This switch-over of our consciousness is the key for deeper healing because:

• The subconscious is the self-appointed protector of the body.

• The subconscious is bigger and has a prompting effect on the conscious.

• The subconscious does not argue, and does not have logic like the conscious mind. It therefore, takes our suggestions, whatever they may be, and implements them through the hypothalamus-Autonomic Nervous System connection.

Pranayama is one of the best methods of healing as it helps the body and activates the subconscious mind. Once the subconscious gets activated, we can expect the sleeping giant within us to awaken and lead us towards higher goals for health and happiness.

We are now ready to communicate and instruct the subconscious mind for healing. The repairing and healing forces of the body can be geared up to combat illness successfully through techniques for strengthening the subconscious mind,. As our skills in self-healing improve, it is possible to speed up the recovery process, and bring joy and vitality back into our life.

In every breath there is a pause. That's when God gives us his silent command. He converses with us that way but only in silence can we listen.

—Anonymous

23

The Power of Words

Affirmations are like prescription for certain aspects of your life you want to change.

—Jerry Frankhauser

Good things come to those who wait, better things come to those who try, the best things come to those who believe.

Affirmations for self-healing

We are what we think. We create our own reality, moment by moment, with the thoughts we choose to think. Our mind expresses and influences our body much more than we can imagine. Thoughts could be called the units of the mind and the foundation of our actions and habits. Words, which are crystallized thoughts, have immeasurable power, especially when we speak them with concentration.

Words powered with emotions influence us throughout the day. The mere thought of fatigue is enough to drain our energy. That exhaustion can be further reinforced by the thought of 'I'm exhausted', which gives definition and adds power to it. The opposite is true, too. If you feel exhausted, but suddenly find your attention drawn to a telephonic talk with a close friend, your fatigue may vanish altogether! If you suddenly spot your maid doing something wrong and are prompted to lose your temper, you'll find the exhaustion is back!

Now, let us observe the usual monologue of suggestions that we usually keep giving to the mind:

- I can't do this.

- I am unlucky.

- It's not my cup of tea.

- People don't care for me.

- I am always wrong.

- I am too old now.

Expressions like 'I can't do this' have a self-sabotaging effect. The subconscious mind is very sensitive to suggestions given to it, and most of our suggestions are in the form of negative words. Our subconscious mind takes us at our word, and sees to it that we cannot, indeed, do a particular thing. It absorbs what is impressed upon it and obediently implements it.

Most of us continue to think the same kind of thoughts, visualize the same mental images, and lead the same kind of life with the same type of health. According to the universal Law of Attraction or the Law of Similars, 'Like attracts like'! It is no wonder that people who always carry dark clouds around with them end up with undesirable experiences, and that positive-minded people keep encountering opportunities and good luck. It is said that any thought consistently held for about 15–20 seconds can attract a similar energy. Is it then surprising that illnesses don't leave us as long as we presume them to be our permanent distressing partners?

Tagging with Disease Names

When suffering from a disease we must not avoid taking the necessary medicines. But paying too much attention to the problem is of no great help, either. By continuously discussing one's ailment with others, we succeed only in giving more energy to the disease since the subconscious registers our fear and the attention we pay to it. By constantly naming the diseases and symptoms, we give them more power over us, thereby suppressing the kinetic energy of healing inside us.

Just as harsh words spoken are never forgotten and the wounds caused thereby remain, similarly the words of doctors too, decide the course of an illness – for example '75 per cent chance of success' has a better impact and subsequent good results than '25 per cent chance of failure'!

To study the power of words, a group of people suffering from the same kind of tumour were given injections of sterile water. The group was divided into two: one group was told they were being given a new drug with no side effects, while the other group was cautioned about its side effects and made to sign a written consent before being given the injection. The first group showed no side effects while the second one reported side effects in the form of loss of hair, appetite and weight.

Choose Your Thoughts and Words

Most of us do not know how to change our way of thinking, or else do not believe that it is possible to do so. We can change the thoughts and images in our mind as easily as we can insert a new DVD into a player and watch a different movie. Fresh thoughts will create fresh events according to their quality and thereby, change our life. By filtering the contents of the mind we can practically experience the creative power that our thoughts possess.

Our thoughts, words and actions can heal or harm. The decision is ours to make – whether we choose to get disturbed or to take calm and correct action. This decision too, is taken in our mind in the form of words, and words can alter our thoughts and mindset! What we tell ourselves is of vital importance. By changing our words and thoughts we can change our life. The strings for controlling our life are in our hands if only we can manage our thoughts and subsequent words. We can use to our advantage the characteristic of the subconscious mind which is to obey, because it merely reacts to suggestions, without arguing or comparing.

It will not happen overnight—reviving the weakened will-power of someone suffering from a chronic disease takes time, the way it takes time to learn new habits. Some time will be required for forming the good habit of 'health consciousness' over 'disease consciousness'.

Affirmations – a Few Words Matter!

An affirmation is a statement that one aspires to absorb into one's life. When repeated with deep concentration, it gets carried into the subconscious, and can change us on those levels of the mind over which most of us do not have much conscious control. Thus, strong, conscious affirmations react on the mind and the body through the medium of the subconscious.

Emile Coué was a French psychologist, who introduced a new method of psychotherapy, self-improvement and healing based on auto-suggestion. His world-famous affirmation, 'Every day, in every way, I am getting better and better', has healed many with serious diseases.

The word affirmation carries with it lot of positive vibes, while the word 'suggestion' or 'self-suggestion' is gentler, implying, as it does, a great degree of freedom and time frame for its implementation, and hence, is more acceptable.

Requirements of the Suggestion

• The suggestion should express 'what we want', not 'what we do not want.' It should be directed at changing ourselves rather than changing another person or happening.

• We should concentrate on positive qualities that are the solutions to our disease and imperfections.

• Words like 'don't' and 'can't' should not be a part of the suggestion. Instead of saying, 'I don't have high blood pressure', it is better to say, 'My blood pressure is coming under control'.

• The suggestion should be in the continuous tense, that is, it should have a progressive quality rather than a static instruction. Instead of 'I do not have acidity', the statement 'My acidity is getting less day by day' is more honest, and would be more acceptable to anyone using it.

• The mental attitude should change from denial and self-hatred to one of trust. The affirmation should be impregnated with will, faith, devotion and belief, unmindful of the results that will come with intensity and repetition.

• One suggestion at a time can be absorbed better than a jargon of confused, multi-tasked phrases.

• The affirmations of our conscious mind become more powerful when they go through the subconscious at the right time x that is, in the optimum state of mind.

• The golden rule is repetition of the suggestion.

If the affirmations are repeated with firmness, strength and deep trust, they will bear results. Success in planting depends on the potency of the seed and the receptivity of the soil; in healing, results depend on the power of the technique and on the receptivity of the subconscious mind. This receptivity comes with trust and faith. So, affirmations should be free of uncertainties and doubts. They should be repeated often, deeply and continuously, till they become a part of our convictions and beliefs.

Attitude of Surrender

When we try to transform ourselves by self-effort alone, we limit our potential for healing and growth. By tuning into the Divine, the Omnipresent Power, that is the source of creativity and solutions, our resistance gets minimized. Our efforts should thus be lifted from our self-enclosure into the greater reality.

Affirmation is only the first step to self-healing. We must do our human best, but, without additional power from the supreme source of power, our efforts will be worthless. Affirmation, in other words, should be done with a prayerful attitude or with an attitude of surrender to the Divine Will. Let us remember that this power to heal is also a gift from the same source.

Preparation

Before making an affirmation, the mind should be free of worries and restlessness. Cast away anxiety and distrust. Acknowledge that the cosmic law is all-powerful and that healing by nature, with faith and concentration, will allow this law to operate unhampered.

Choose or frame your affirmation, and write it in a notebook. Repeat it first loudly, then softly and more slowly till the voice becomes a whisper. Then gradually affirm it mentally until you can feel it as an unbroken continuous thought. Avoid mechanical repetition. Repeating it firmly, with intensity and sincerity, will take it to your core, whence it will return later with the power to influence your conscious realm.

Blackboard Technique

Many have successfully used this technique to improve health and to resolve problems. Imagine a blackboard and take an imaginary piece of chalk. Then write on the blackboard what you desire, or the lingering question in your mind. By practising daily the writing on the blackboard, one tries to visualize the words as clearly as possible.

Sample Affirmations

For Better Health

• Day by day, in every way, my issue / problem is coming under control.

  • I am getting better day by day.
  • My strength and health are improving daily.
  • I love myself and my body.
  • I choose to heal, I am on the right path, I feel great.
  • I choose to release the emotional cause of my problem.
  • I choose my ——————— to feel healthy and fine.
  • I choose to let the pain go.
  • Every cell in my body is regaining health and harmony.

For Self-Improvement

• I leave behind me both my failures and accomplishments; what I do today will create a new and better future, filled with inner joy.

• I choose to release my past and step into the future.

• Whatever I do in life, I give it my full attention.

• Like a laser beam, I burn all problems, all obstructions that are in front of me!

• Negative thoughts and suggestions have no influence over me.

• I make a difference wherever I go.

• I see opportunity in every challenge.

• I choose to ignore _____ and get my power back.

• I am infused with the energy of well-being.

• I am ready to move ahead in life.

• I choose to have a great day.

• I choose to attract good things to me.

When we consciously speak of a positive quality, it gains power and can become a valuable treasure.

24

The Power of Visualization – Imagery

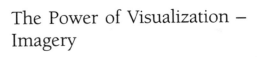

Chance favours only the prepared mind.

—Louis Pasteur

You can't depend on your eyes when your imagination is out of focus.

—Mark Twain

Using biofeedback for healing

The Healing Power of Attention and Images

You must have often wondered why you seem to get a mental picture of something while reading a book or indulging in a daydream. This ability of the mind to create vivid image forms from our thoughts is known as imagery. The Yogic Sutras address imagery as *Vikalpa* or a fragment or a form of a wave of consciousness that has its source in the heart.

A mental image is the experience of perceiving an object, an event, or a scene, when the relevant object, event, or scene is not actually visible to the senses. Some people are more visual-oriented while others can feel things better. Some people can think in words, such as musicians who, on hearing a song, can sometimes 'see' the song notes in their head. So imagery is not strictly visual, and perception can come through any sense – sight, smell, taste, feel or sound. Think about experiences such as recalling the smell of the ocean breeze or of the first rain showers, or music that reminds you of a loved one, or the surge of energy that accompanies an achievement! We actually freeze our thoughts and words as images throughout the day and even in sleep. Our dreams reflect the state of our mind.

Images Have Power

Sensory images have power – reading a recipe book produces saliva in the mouth as images form in the mind of the look, the taste and the texture of food. On the other hand, the thought of a past sickness can induce nausea, cramps in the stomach, chills or fatigue. Educational researchers have observed that by merely imagining doing a five-finger piano exercise – mental practice – resulted in a significant improvement in performance, as compared to no mental practice. Researchers have concluded that *'Mental practice alone seems to be sufficient to promote the modulation of neural circuits involved in the early stages of motor skill learning'.*

Sigmund Freud, the pioneer in behaviour therapy, believed that mental images that formed in the subconscious according to latent desires have a major influence on human behaviour and health. Vivid imagery results in a message being sent to the emotional control centre of the brain. From there, the message is passed along to the body's endocrine, immune and Autonomic Nervous Systems, thus influencing a wide range of bodily functions and health.

It's all about attitude again! If we look at our wrinkles every morning, we will look for wrinkles in others too, but if we look for positivity around us, positivity will flow into us.

Words form images in the mind, and the images influence body functions. A group of people was shown a film that featured Mother Teresa lovingly stroking spastic children, who, as a result, sat smiling and relaxed in her lap. The functions of the immune system of the audience were checked twice – before and after the movie. Although the audience previously had held varying opinions about Mother Teresa, there was a rise in the immune functions of all. The soft emotions triggered by the film instantaneously boosted immune status!

Imagery for Health and Healing

Aristotle and Hippocrates believed that images in the brain had the power to enliven the body and the mind. Today, research has proved that they were right. Guided imagery, which has now been accepted as an emerging science, is used to help patients use the full range of the body's healing capacity. In fact, imagery is a very potent instrument that helps us make autosuggestions, that is, suggestions to the self. Using this biofeedback, people have been helped to reduce elevated blood pressure, control irregular heartbeats, eliminate migraine headaches, cure sleeplessness, and to aid many functions of the body.

In the words of Dr. Barbara Brown, a pioneer in biofeedback research: 'If some medical researchers are now teaching hearts, or the minds of hearts, to reverse a pathological condition, then medicine must be learning that relationships between mind and body are more powerful than they had once thought; research into biofeedback is the first medically testable indication that the *mind can relieve illnesses as well as create them.*'

Images are the true language of the mind, something that it understands immediately. We can characterize our imagery to various degrees with our conscious control. The good news is that we can deliberately introduce positive healthful images. Research findings show how physical changes can occur in the body as a result of self-engineered imagery:

• An increase in the number of white blood cells and neutrophils (cells of the immune system) at the sight of infection

• Heightened levels of Immunoglobulin A in the saliva (an indicator of heightened level of immune functions)

• Elimination of the standard histamine response, such as itching, redness and blisters, to an allergen – poison ivy – when taken for a harmless plant. Conversely, blisters appear when a harmless plant is taken to be poison ivy.

• Managing headaches – imagery helps reduce the frequency of migraine headaches as effectively as taking preventive medication.

• Patients with serious burns who used imagery experienced less pain and used fewer painkillers.

• Reduction of the aversion response to chemotherapy in cancer patients

• Positive imagery before surgery speeds up post-surgical recovery and ensures a shorter duration of hospital stay.

• Playing recorded audiotapes during surgery reduces the requirement of morphine as an anaesthetic agent.

Dr. David Spiegel, renowned psychiatrist at Stanford University, carried out a study on the effects of relaxing imagery on a group of patients with metastatic (spread in body) breast cancer. On a follow-up a year later, the group that had been practising imagery reported less pain and had better control. After ten years, that group had, on an average, lived longer than the ones who had not practised imagery.

Types of Imagery

Eliciting the right image can be done using different techniques which would depend on what appeals to an individual and what the aim behind it is.

Basic Imagery

This is the simplest form of imagery and can be done by anyone for feeling relaxed or changing the mood. It can produce significant results, as proved by Dr. David Spiegel in his study on cancer patients, where participants imagined themselves floating very gently in water and, as a result, felt relaxed and peaceful.

One method of practising this sort of imagery is to let the imagination take us to our favourite place – a garden, a special retreat, the beach, the mountains. Let your imagination soar as you try to relive the experience.

Breath-cleansing Imagery

Our breaths can be used to unlock the power of imaging. In a standard exercise, one focuses the attention on the breaths, imagining that with each inhalation, the life- giving energy is nourishing the diseased, or painful or stiff part of the body, cleansing and massaging it, with the exhalations, the discomfort is getting less.

Colour Imagery

One can add colours to make the above imagery more effective – clean, white air being inhaled by the diseased part, and greyish-brown air being exhaled, symbolizing the release of the pain and discomfort with the exhaled air.

Outcome Imagery

This a very simple form of imagery where the person visualizes the desired result, imagining himself or herself as being already in the condition that he or she wishes for. One does not need to have any technical information to do this type of imagery. An obese individual can visualize himself or herself as being thin, feeling very energetic, full of joy, dressed in a long-desired outfit. A patient with arthritis can visualize freedom and lightness of movement with flexible and pain-free joints. Athletes at the Olympic Games are made to do this type of imagery before they compete in an event.

Physiological Imagery

Physiological imagery requires a basic understanding of how things work in our body, and the mechanism that has created the disease condition in us. It then involves visualizing the desired physiological processes in the body that will lead to better health. Heart attacks and angina pains are due to the narrowing of blood vessels in the heart with fatty plaques. One can use physiological imagery to 'see' the blood vessels flexible and clear, and the blood flowing freely without any hindrance. One can feel the arteries as being smooth so that nothing can stick on the walls to produce any blockage.

Cellular Imagery

Cellular imagery requires an understanding of the way the cells work in the body. It is very effective as it targets the cellular site where the root activity takes place. This type of imagery is very satisfying for the biologically-oriented mind. Others may find it complicated unless it is explained by a doctor with the help of pictures. For example, a doctor can guide a patient to imagine natural killer cell activity at the site of a tumour.

Fantasized Imagery

To make the cellular and the physiological imagery more understandable and easy to imagine, one can expand the imagination and simplify the content of the imagery. In the above example of cellular imagery, one can visualize the killer cells as soldiers with guns in their hands firing on the tumour, or sharks surrounding the tumour and destroying it: the resultant healing can actually be felt.

25

Practising Imagery

Imagination is more important than knowledge.

—Albert Einstein

Ultimately, there can be no complete healing until we have restored our primal trust in life.

—Georg Feuerstein

Techniques for self-suggestion

Images in the mind are real events for the body, and they can help to heal. What happens with effective imagery is that willpower, along with the imagination, stimulates the life force into rushing to a diseased part and healing it. Take the example of a dumb person who, in response to a fire in his building, shouted 'Fire, fire'! The strong desire to survive took over his subconscious mind and he was able to speak out! Other examples include paralysed arms regaining strength, or the return of a paralysed person's voice when he tried to sing! Imagery helps produce more alpha waves that assist the inner resources for healing.

Guided Imagery vs. Self-practice

Guided imagery or supervised imagery with live instructions, or with the help of an audiotape, is the common mode of practice. Some people are more comfortable practising imagery on their own in familiar surroundings. Providing them with pre-recorded guided instructions is not very practical as they have to make a purely 'beta' effort to switch on the device, adjust the volume, etc. All this dilutes the state of relaxed internal attention.

Optimum State of Mind

Imagery works better when introduced in the optimum state of mind, because it is a state of relaxed focus with energized alertness and heightened sensitivity. Here, we are capable of more rapid and intense healing, learning and positive change. It allows us to go beyond what we normally think of as there being a 'kind of flow in the zone'. This same principle is used to train sportsmen and athletes to go beyond their normal levels of achievement. They are made to visualize reaching their targets or goal.

Pranayama helps us reach this optimum state. It not only cleanses and energizes the body but also produces the optimum state so that deeper healing can take place. Truly, breaths are the bridge between the body and the mind.

Effective Imagery

Points to be kept in mind:

- Imagery is fun.

- Anyone can do it; there are no side effects.

- It is a useful supplement to medical treatment.

- You don't have to memorize anything.

- Allow, don't force – let your feelings come from the heart.

- Enjoy the freedom to be creative and get the maximum benefits.

- Indulge when in a relaxed frame of mind.

- Precede the imagery with pranayama.

- It is not necessary to be very objective about the physiological image you want to create: there is no need to worry about the minute details of the picture, just understanding the concept is enough. Ultimately we have to feel it rather than merely visualize it.

• If you find it difficult to feel or visualize, just let your positive mental dialogue with the subconscious mind continue.

• Create, visualize, feel, enjoy the magic and the power!

• Persistence and regularity pay.

• Just let your mind 'see' what it wants; feel it with joy and a sense of having done it, and you will!

• Do not jump out of the session – let it be a smooth transition

When should I practise?

The ideal time is the first thing in the morning or during the conscious calmness that precedes sleep at night. There is no hard and fast rule however; depending on convenience, you can engage in imagery at any time as long as you are in the least distracted state of mind. Many find it more enjoyable and fruitful when they are free of daily chores, maybe in the early afternoon hours or evening. Scheduling the sessions at the same time every day is important, too.

At times we may need a sort of 'SOS' session – a short one to clear the mind, or whenever we feel the need, that is, whenever our attention drifts towards our problems. It is worthwhile to consciously replace the thoughts of fear, anxiety about a problem or disease with a positive suggestion or image with faith and will.

Where should I practise?

Choose a pleasant quiet place where you will not be disturbed. To prevent disturbances turn the cell phone off or put it in silent mode, switch off the doorbell, have someone to handle external calls. If the sound of traffic cannot be avoided, play some soft and soothing classical or instrumental music. To avoid falling asleep do not practise imagery after a heavy meal.

Posture while practising

For guided sessions under supervision lie down flat on your back. For self-practice you can sit in any position – in a straight-backed chair, or on the floor in any of several poses. Two things, however, are essential: your spine must be straight, and you must be able to relax completely. The preceding practices of pranayama are usually done sitting, and help to keep us well tuned into the desired state of mind.

How does it work?

Visualizing colour: When we eat too much, we feel lazy; similarly, when the mind has to take in too much, it too gets blocked. Too much of anything is bad and we have to develop a harmonious equilibrium between taking and giving. Visualizing colours during breathing dissolves this 'congestion' in the mind, and restores the energy flow of the body. Like a pressure relief valve, we breathe out the excess and start the natural flow of energy in ourselves.

Running a movie: A relaxed permissive atmosphere allows the subconscious to receive images. This 'attitude of allowing' is best encouraged when the imagery is made to run like a movie in the mind. This sort of movie is usually experienced as a hodge podge that keeps changing in intensity, so don't expect it to be like a regular film.

Images as per our value system: Imagery works better when the images chosen are in tune with our way of thinking. Warlike images of immune system cells killing a tumour will not be congruent with a priest who preaches non-violence. However the same technique can show dramatic results with a young teenager!

Eliciting emotions: Imagery is a right brain activity where our emotions co-exist. Because of this, imagery that elicits emotions can be more powerful. Rather than running the image mechanically, trying to feel the joy of the desired result would have a deeper impact, and may at times elicit tears and a feeling of being deeply touched.

Magical touch: The power of touch deeply affects one and all. During the practice of imagery, touching the part that needs healing could be the most powerful accompaniment. Touching helps in directing awareness to the appropriate places in the body. For example asthmatics can put their hands on the chest as they visualize the airways of the lungs opening and clearing.

- Touching helps to settle the restlessness of the monkey mind.

- The images become clearer and more vivid with contact, making them more intense and powerful.

- Touching the desired parts can invoke intense positive emotions of self-love, care and gratitude towards the healing forces.

Experiencing imagery: A purely flat, two-dimensional imagery, with the help of line diagrams, was found less effective with people who aren't particularly 'visual'. For maximum impact, the imagery has to be felt or experienced in the body. The more sensory the imaging, the greater are its effects. For example, a hypertensive can visualize blood flowing more freely, without any obstacles, in blood vessels that are clear and supple.

Coming out of the session: It is advisable not to open the eyes suddenly, but rather, proceed gently from the subtle to the gross. During imagery we operate in the realm of the mind and its dimensions. So before opening our eyes, we have to proceed from mind awareness to breath awareness to body awareness. Taking a few deep breaths brings breath awareness; follow this with small movements in different parts of the body such as rolling the shoulders, opening and closing the fingers, turning the head from one side to the other, etc. This brings back body awareness. Slowly proceed to opening the eyes with a few blinks.

Techniques

For ease of practice, various mental imaging techniques have been described under two broad headings—general and problem specific. Choose any one or combine several from different categories.

A. Common Imagery

1. Imagery for Stress Relief

As stress is the root cause of most of our common problems, these techniques can be applied by anyone. Visualize yourself enjoying nature in any place of your choice.

The sea beach: Smell the light breeze ... feel the gentle cool air touching your skin ... look out at the vast expanse of the sea ... listen to the sound of waves crashing on to the shore ... imagine yourself lying down on the beach ... the warm sand below you ... you are safe, away from the big waves ...

Hot air balloon: You are in a hot air balloon high up in the air ... you can see the city spread out below you ... the roads ... the houses ... the people moving around going about their lives ... the day-to-day problems below cannot disturb you ... cannot affect you ... there are no demands on you ... you are just yourself ... content, satisfied and at peace ...

A feather flying: You are a feather – soft, pure, white ... flowing with the soothing breeze ... gently floating down ... slowly descending ... you feel more and more relaxed as it gets closer to the ground ... the feather gently touches the ground, and you are fully relaxed ...

Water flowing: Put all your self-criticism, negativity, anxiety and worries on a boat or a raft, push it away gently into the water ...

A rose blossoming: You are a beautiful rosebud, red or pink or white ... any colour you like ... a fresh bud with the morning dew drops glistening on it ... now imagine the petals opening ... slowly ... one by one ... as each petal unfurls, your body gets relaxed ... you release all the tightness and tension from the body ... part by part ... face and neck ... arms ... chest ... abdomen ... back ... hips and thighs ... legs ... feet ... as the rose petals keep opening feel the wave of relaxation and wellness take over completely ... feel that you are the rose ... radiant with inner and outer beauty and health ...

A happy moment: Visualize a happy incident from your life ... run it like a movie ... how you look ... what you are wearing ... the people around you ... the details of that happening ... how happy you are ... live the incident all over again ...

2. Imagery for Cleansing

Cleansing the body

Imagine that the air you are breathing is pure and bright, and as you inhale, a stream of golden light from the universe flows into you. It makes you feel fresh and good. Breathe it into all the parts of your body, one after the other—toes, feet, legs, knees, thighs, hips, lower back, abdomen, chest, hands, arms, shoulders, neck, face, and head. Feel the warm light flow into your body, let every cell bathe in it. As you continue breathing, allow your body to dissolve completely in the golden light, allowing every part of the body to release and relax.

Having established contact with each part of the body, listen to what it needs. Exhale the tension and pain there is in any part of the body like a black stream, maintaining awareness in that part. For poor functioning, send bright golden energy into the affected part. Weak points get strengthened and harmonized by consciously breathing golden light into them.

Cleansing the mind

When you exhale, let a heavy, stream of black air flow out of your nose, releasing all your heavy thoughts and anxieties. Negative emotions and feelings should be exhaled in a calm manner with the firm conviction that no emotions are permanent. Visualize the black stream of negativity going far away into the universe.

3. Imagery for Energization

You are the sun: The sun is the all-pervading source of universal energy. Visualize yourself watching the sunrise on the horizon ... the vibrant rays diffusing across the morning sky ... imagine the sun in your heart region ... the rays are spreading inside your body ... a sense of warmth ... feel it in your body ... feel the strength ... feel the rays of energy spreading all around your body ... you are full of vitality ... your inner sun is very powerful and gives you all the energy for health ...

A golden ball of light: Imagine a ball of light over your head ... the golden light enters your body through the crown of the head ... flowing down slowly like a liquid ... bathing each part of your body as it descends ... face ... neck ... shoulders, arms and chest ... upper abdomen ... lower abdomen ... hips ... thighs ... knees ... legs ... and the feet ... the entire body is light and luminous ... filled with energy ... all charged up ... the skin glows as the body pulsates with renewed energy ...

A waterfall: You are lying at the foot of a very gentle waterfall ... with cool clear water trickling over your face ... softly refreshing you ... you come out of the waterfall with your skin fresh ... cleansed ... tingling ... glowing ... shining ...

4. Imagery for Pain Relief

Pain is a very subjective symptom. The degree of pain one experiences depends on the mindset of an individual. An injury of the same intensity in the same part of the body has been found to produce intense pain in a person who is always scared of falling sick, while it produces much less pain in a person who is mentally stronger and positive in attitude.

Medicines may have to be taken for injuries, but these additional practices will speed the recovery and reduce the intensity of the pain. The following methods show very good results when the pain is predominantly born out of stress or due to anxiety or worry.

Touch method: Keeping the eyes closed, gently place one palm on the painful part ... repeat the words in your mind, 'it is going away, it is going away...' till the pain becomes less and gradually disappears!

Colour breath imagery: With eyes closed, focus your attention on the breaths ... observe the inhalations and the exhalations ... smooth, rhythmic, easy breaths ... feel tuned in to your breaths ... now think of the painful part of your body as you continue breathing ... visualize the painful part breathing ... as you inhale, golden air with life- giving energy is entering the painful or stiff part ... cleansing it ... the discomfort gets released with the greyish-brown air getting exhaled from that area ... continue visualizing this as the breaths keep coming and going. Feel the body light and luminous as the pain gets less, and the body gets energized with the breaths.

Colour imagery: With eyes closed, focus your attention on the breaths ... observe the inhalations and the exhalations ...smooth, rhythmic, easy breaths ... feel tuned in to your breaths ... now think of the painful part of your body as you continue breathing ... think of the painful part as a black patch ... as you continue to breathe naturally, the black colour becomes less and less till it regains the normal skin colour. Feel the body light and luminous as the pain gets less, and the body gets energized with the breaths.

B. Problem Specific Imagery

Slipped disc/back ache

Take your awareness to that part of your back which hurts ... breathe with ease as you feel the breaths moving in and out from the painful part ... the air coming in is fresh and white ... the air going out is brown as it is taking away the pain with it ... visualize a good healthy disc in the space cushioning the two adjacent bones of your spinal cord ... there is no compression on the nerve coming from the side ... feel the muscles of that part and your back relaxed ... as the tension dissolves, the back feels better ... feel your posture improving ... feel the ease of your movements ... feel your back regaining strength.

Skin disease

Visualize the skin as normal and healthy, and do the imagery technique for pain relief, substituting the diseased skin with the painful part. Progressively using the breaths, visualize the skin becoming normal ... glowing ... radiant ... fresh ... younger ...

Obesity

See yourself as you want to look, fitter and slimmer, and wearing a particular outfit ... visualize yourself receiving compliments for the achievement from close friends and family ... imagine how confident and elated you are feeling ... you are running with ease on the sea shore ... full of enthusiasm ... now visualize the food you should be eating ... review your diet ... what to eat ... how much to eat ... select the between-meal snacks ... tell yourself that this is the food your body needs ... tell your body not to send waves of craving for foods that should not be eaten ... look again at yourself ... see the new look ...

Heart disease and hypertension

All the practices under the heading of relaxation do wonders for the heart! You can choose any of them. Here is one specifically for the heart:

Bring your awareness to the heart region ... place one palm over it ... become aware of your breaths ... see your heart working non-stop for you ... feel the connection with your heart ... the heart works with greater ease ... see your heart smiling ... pumping blood with ease ... now see the blood flowing easily in a wide and smooth blood vessel ... no obstacles, no blockages ... your heart is beating steadily, nourishing the entire body ... your heart is getting stronger ... visualize yourself moving around with ease, without getting any chest pain ... comfortable, calm.

Migraine

Imagine a black band wrapped tight around your forehead ... feel the squeezing sensation and the discomfort ... feel the

throbbing sensation ... you have to get rid of this black band
that is causing the pain ... now imagine the band breaking,
falling off ... the pressure on your head too, gives way ... the
tension and the pain slowly dissolve and disappear ... you
decide to fling the band far away ... the pain goes ... you feel
light and relieved ... say in your mind, 'I release all my tensions
and feel light and calm'... visualize the blood flowing freely
through the blood vessels of your forehead ...

Asthma

Place your hands on your chest to sense the movement of air ...
focus on your breaths ... observe the natural rhythm of your
breathing ... now take deeper breaths ... inhale through your
nose ... exhale gently through your mouth ... maintain the
rhythm ... visualze your bronchial tubes ... the air going in and
coming out through the tubes as you breathe ... your bronchial
tubes are relaxed ... there is no spasm ... no tightness in the
tubes ... unobstructed, the air is moving ... feel your lungs
filling up with air ... pink lungs ... all healthy ... feel the
confident you breathing naturally and with ease ... visualize
yourself running, walking with ease ... your breathing is
comfortable ... feel your chest move easily as you breathe—no
tightness, no spasm ...

Diabetes

Place your hands in the hollow of your abdomen just below the
chest bone in the midline ... visualize your pancreas there ...
yellow-coloured glucose particles moving in the blood ... the
hungry cells in the body needing insulin to take in this glucose
for energy ... now feel your pancreas releasing red-coloured
insulin particles into the blood ... this insulin allows the yellow
glucose to enter the cells ... it eases the hunger of the cells in the
body for glucose ...

Fracture and injury

Visualize the two ends of the fractured bone ... place your hand
gently there ... feel extra blood reaching there to heal ... feel the

warmth ... the edges of the broken bone are getting interwoven and knitted together ... new cells are filling up the tiny gaps like cement ... there are white blood cells in that area to keep all infections away ... now visualize yourself using that part of the body with ease.

Arthritis

The two common types of arthritis are osteoarthritis and rheumatoid arthritis. To reduce the friction in the joint space, there is a padding of cartilage on the approximating bone surfaces. In osteoarthritis, there is addition of material to the bone, thus reducing the space. In rheumatoid arthritis there is erosion of the cartilage and swelling of the soft tissues around the joint.

In continuation of the imagery under the pain section ... visualize the joint space ... feel a healthy covering of cartilage on the surface of the bones ... there is no erosion ... no extra bone growth ... the surrounding muscles are healthy, soft, supple ...

Cancer

Take your awareness to the site of the growth ... your immune cells have enough strength to attack the tumour and destroy it ... visualize your immune cells to be a noble army of soldiers with guns ... they shatter the tumour ...

Or ... picture the immune cells to be like sharks ... surrounding your cancer, which is like a school of weak fish ... the sharks engulf the fish and gulp them down ... feel yourself full of strength ...

Twenty minutes a day can change your life!

Spend just twenty minutes every day on imagery. This time-investment will go a long way towards making you healthier, happier and more productive. We have been given will-power, concentration, faith, reason and common sense to use when trying to rid our self of bodily and mental afflictions. All these powers should be employed like a trump card, an unbeatable advantage that we can use any time. Let us make it happen!

26

Healing U-Turns

Seek not abroad, turn back into thyself, for in the inner man dwells the truth.

—St. Augustine

One cannot tell when he is going to be healed, so do not try to set an exact time limit, Faith, not time, will determine when the cure will be effected.

—Paramhansa Yogananda

Going from the outside to the inside

Our eyes perceive only what is on the surface, and we believe that we can comprehend everything with our intelligence. But that's not the whole story. Our body, the entire physiology of our system, is permanently over-stimulated. Our fast-paced life and our non-stop thoughts take a toll on our health.

Lifestyle management strategies like exercising, dietary overhaul, 'conscious' eating habits, pleasure-giving hobbies like music, dance, etc., all help us enjoy a better state of health. Despite that, sickness remains or in other words, why don't healthy individuals get sick? The assumption of experts that healthy people have good genes or are simply lucky is no more than a half-truth. The healthiest people in society actually fall into a different profile altogether.

People who are able to stay clear of diseases, or who live up to old age without major illnesses are those who practise emotional adaptability. They are the ones who, despite any crisis in life, can bounce back and look towards the future instead of dwelling in the past. Such people practise good coping mechanisms which are the key to adaptability. A time-tested, simple yet profound, coping mechanism is Pranayama, which can help us at all levels – physical, physiological, emotional and psychological.

Things that really matter in life seldom announce their value, and one such very vital aspect of our existence and health is our breathing. We neglect tapping into its powers because breathing silently takes care of itself. We take it for granted, forgetting that our breathing is inseparable from prana, the subtle life energy that sustains and maintains the body, and is the force behind the functions of the mind. Breath- management actually provides us with an opportunity to access our inherent capacity to heal ourselves.

By regulating our breaths, we can influence our nervous system. Breathing is the foundation of all emotional influences upon the body. When breathing is in a state of equilibrium, our emotions too, get balanced. By breathing attentively, we can establish a relationship with all parts of the body. Pranayamic breathing techniques thus offer a highway to holistic health. This highway could be said to have two pathways – the outer and the inner.

The outer pathway is through its beneficial effects on the body as tools for cleansing, detoxification, energizing, and rejuvenation. The body develops resilience as the energy channels become increasingly free and sensitive, allowing vital energy to stream through them. The first almost immediate effect of the regular practice of pranayama is a tremendous boost in the levels of our energy, and a sense of well-being and immense enrichment. Pranayama is like a via media for unending fuel to the body.

The inner pathway works on our thoughts and feelings. We have set traps for ourselves that prevent us from coming out of our sufferings. As long as we believe in the compulsive deterioration of our body, the body will continue to remain sick. If we can let go of the negative thoughts and, instead, nurture positive healing thoughts and images, the disease process can be given a 'U-turn'! Our mind has merely to change the image of our self. This will help the mind get rid of old concepts, and accumulate new ideas in their place. Mental control can be achieved by reining in the breaths because the breaths link the body and the mind. Pranayama then creates a congenial milieu for the mind to get consciously re-programmed towards health and happiness.

Both the pathways – the inner and the outer – are connected with each other. Ultimately, the secret of pranayama is its power to transform both the body and the mind. Breathing actually corresponds to taking charge of one's own life, and self-mastery is the DNA of life mastery.

One of the ways of blocking healing is to say 'no' to ourselves. The number of small ways in which we become mean, and often, unknowingly, we deprive ourselves of a lot of joy in life, is astonishing. So please, let go of any possible unpleasant connotation that the word 'healing' may have for you. Instead, open up to its actual meaning. True understanding happens through experiencing, not through words. The best things in life have to be felt from the heart. Feel from your core with a deep inner motivation, and carry on with inspiration. Open yourself up to this healing adventure.

I am not talking of wonders here. Every bit of matter is part of a cycle of decay and death. But with these practices, you can slow down the processes. Our mind is more flexible and receptive than we believe, and it actually wants to be challenged. We just need to reorient ourselves.

We have been groomed in the fast-paced world of today to have whatever we desire and that too, right away. If something does not work out, our patience gets exhausted. What appeared to be important merely a moment ago, is quickly discarded. Philosophy has comprehended the wisdom of patience – anything to be done well cannot be done quickly! Time spent on pranayama never goes waste as it is time well expended. With daily practice, one is endowed with unbelievable stamina, energy and longevity, within a few days.

Getting up every morning just fifteen minutes before your usual time will create space for the regular practice of the three basic pranayamas – the cleansing and stimulating Kapalabhati, the balancing and energizing Nadi Shuddhi Pranayama, and the calming and rejuvenating Bhramari. With their integration into your everyday life, you will regain your inner poise and harmony, and you will enjoy resting calmly in your own centre. Your emotional equilibrium will get reset after the 'vacation effect' of the practices. You will then be thankful for the effectiveness of these exercises. With persistent practice, the pleasant moments will get intensified and extensive in the course of time.

Embrace change – sometimes in the winds of change we find our true direction! We can either remain vulnerable, victimized and hopeless, or favourably change our internal milieu – both body and mind.

As long as we meet our life with openness, we will keep moving towards positivity and harmony. Life should be fun and should bring joy. We should aim at being happy and satisfied for only then can we have a positive effect on our environment. This book sets down guidelines on how to use our breathing advantageously. It is now up to us to make use of them. Let us put our trust in life and healing, and get comfortable with our own self.

I would like to conclude with the words of Abraham Lincoln:

'And in the end, it's not the years in your life that counts. It's the life in your years.'

To be comfortable with oneself is to be comfortable with the world.

   • Give up irresponsible living and take action by choosing to live a healthy life.

- Treat your body with love and care.

- Breathe with awareness.

- Look inward and find your balance.

- Listen to the small voice that whispers to you when you are in need of an answer.

- Interact with people who are positive and interested in continuous improvement, not with people who have a negative attitude, hate themselves, and are waiting for things to happen for them.

- Challenge your core beliefs and replace them with new encouraging self-talk.

- Adopt mental 'housekeeping' strategies of gratefulness, forgiveness, and acceptance of the unchangeable.

- Do the best you can in your field of work and life.

- A righteous life and transparent living generate healing energies.

Self-possessed, resolute act
Without any thought of results,
Open to success or failure,
This equanimity is Yoga.

—Bhagavad Gita (2.48)

FAQ's about the Practice of Pranayama

Answers to some basic questions about the practice of pranayama

Can a total novice practise pranayama?

A big **YES!** Some authorities believe that pranayama should be started only after the asanas have been mastered. Others affirm that the practice of pranayama and asanas should be done simultaneously. In actuality, you need not wait to practise pranayama till you have full mastery over the asanas. You can practice asanas and pranayama side by side. In course of time, you will acquire perfection in both. As long as you can breathe, you can do pranayama.

Which should be done first – asana or pranayama?

Asanas or, for that matter, any form of physical exercise like walking, should ideally be done before the practice of pranayama. The aim is to progress from the gross to the subtle, the breath being subtler than the body. The practice of pranayama leads to a subtler plane – the mind. Doing exercise after pranayama will defeat this deeper purpose of doing pranayama.

Why should we breathe through one nostril, then the other, when the air ultimately has to go to the lungs?

Right-nostril breathing, governed by the Sympathetic Nervous System (SNS), corresponds with the left side of the brain, and its attributes of logic, reason, intellect and reason. The left nostril, governed by the Parasympathetic Nervous System (PNS), corresponds with the right side of the brain, and its attributes of coolness, intuition, feelings, peace and awareness. Breathing through them alternately stimulates both halves of the brain, thus creating an inner balance of our mental faculties.

Should people with hypertension and heart diseases do Kapalabhati?

Yes, they may, but the practice should be done at a slower pace without producing any strain or a feeling of suffocation. It is advisable to do small and slow rounds of the practice with breaks in-between.

How does pranayama relax the body and the mind?

The respiratory rate is directly proportional to the Basal Metabolic Rate (BMR), the rate at which we spend energy to carry out the basal functions of the body. With pranayama, we consciously bring the respiratory rate down, thus reducing the BMR. The amount of reduction in the BMR is a measure of the rest that the system is getting. Slowing down the breath provides a very deep rest for both the body and the mind.

Prolonging the exhalations triggers the Parasympathetic Nervous System (PNS) which eases and releases the stress by balancing out the 'fight-and-flight' response to stress mediated by the PNS.

How does pranayama energize?

In our fast and over-reactive life, we spend 1,500 to 2,000 calories for our basic functions. If we regularly practise pranayama for about 30 minutes daily, we will need only 500-1,000 calories for the same basic bodily functions. The body learns to use the resources more economically. As a result, more energy remains unused and makes us feel energized and enthusiastic throughout the day.

If pranayama conserves energy, will I put on weight while doing pranayama?

Not really! We need to strike the right balance. That is why a pranayama session starts with kriyas like Kapalabhati and Bhastrika, which increase the BMR (Basal Metabolic Rate), and also rid the body of carbon dioxide. Secondly, regular practice of pranayama helps control hunger pangs, thus preventing us from overeating and bingeing as well.

How do Kapalabhati and Bhastrika relax the mind when they are stimulating in effect?

Kapalabhati and Bhastrika do lead to an increased tone in the Sympathetic Nervous System (SNS), which is stimulating for the body and the mind, and thus invigorates both. During the pause at the end of these practices (Kewal Kumbhaka), there is a parasympathetic overtone that relaxes the mind.

Why should Kapalabhati be done first?

Water cannot flow freely through a blocked pipe until the blockage is cleared. If we want to redecorate a room we get rid of the existing furniture before moving in the new furniture. Similarly, we need to cleanse the body of toxins like carbon dioxide, before bringing in fresh air. The active exhalations of Kapalabhati transport the impurities from the body, making more room for the oxygen and prana to enter.

Is it safe for us to practise Kumbhaka?

Many years ago, when pranayama and yoga were a way of life in India, attaining Kewal Kumbhaka was easy through mastery of the breath ratios. The bliss of Kumbhaka could be experienced without straining the body and the mind.

Today most of us lead a sedentary life. Living with the help of machines at all levels as we do, our breaths are curtailed and very shallow. Aiming for Kumbhaka at the beginning of pranayama is unadvisable; people often complain of headaches, eyestrain, migraines and even asthma. If we experience strain or exertion during the pauses, we expend energy, and this prevents us from enjoying the sequence. Thus it is necessary to be minimally strained during the pause.

You should attempt Kumbhaka only under a trained teacher, and do it along with the bandhas. You must be able to breathe comfortably for 5-10 minutes with a ratio of 10:20 between the inhalation and the exhalation.

Can deep-breathing help a person quit smoking?

Deep-breathing is one of the best practices to help people quit smoking. Instead of reaching for a hot toxic gulp of air, it is better to inhale a breath of fresh air, which is oxygenated and energized. If only smokers could take a deep breath without the smoke, they would feel great! A smoker can get the same satisfaction with a gulp of fresh air. Deep inhalation gives him time to think and assess the situation. Slowly and surely he will be able to gain control over the mind.

A Practical Routine

A Stepwise Approach to Pranayama

1. Recognition of our breathing imbalances:

   • Shallow erratic breathing

   • Small inhalations with smaller exhalations

   • Reverse or paradoxical breathing patterns

2. Correcting faulty breathing habits:

   • Stretching and breathing exercises

   • Conscious breathing to correct the excessive speed, jerks and randomness of breathing

   • Abdominal breathing to correct paradoxical breathing

3. Cleansing breaths to reduce the toxic overload in the body and correct faulty breathing habits:

   • Kapalabhati

   • Bhastrika

4. Pranayama to increase sensitivity, bring balance and slow down the breath:

   • Anuloma Viloma Pranayama and Nadi Shuddhi Pranayama

- Ujjayi Pranayama

5. Pranayama to expand awareness:

- Bhramari

- OM chanting

6. Mental Programming

Daily Practice of Pranayama

Here's how to go about your daily practice of pranayama:

Prayer

Settle down in the posture in which you are most at ease. Start with a prayerful attitude.

Kapalabhati Kriya (Cleansing Breath)

- Basic principle – active and forceful exhalation and passive inhalation

- Exhalation – force the air out with active flapping movements of the abdomen in quick succession (but never at the risk of getting breathless). Rate of exhalation initially is slower – 50-60/min, which increases comfortably to 100-120/min with time and practice.

- Inhalation – passive, by relaxing the abdominal muscles at the end of each exhalation

- After one minute, stop the practice. In the initial stages you can stop earlier.

- There should be an automatic suspension of breathing on stopping Kapalabhati. Simultaneously, the mind may experience a deep state of silence. Enjoy this state of deep rest and freshness.

- Wait until the breathing becomes normal.

Anuloma Viloma Nadi Shuddhi Pranayama (Alternate-Nostril Breathing)

• Lightly close the right nostril with the right thumb and exhale completely through the left nostril. Then inhale completely through the left nostril.

• Gently close the left nostril with the ring and the little finger and release the right nostril. Now exhale completely and slowly through the right nostril.

• Inhale deeply through the same (right) nostril then close the right and exhale through the left nostril. This completes one round of Nadi Shuddhi Pranayama.

• Initially, establish a 1:1 ratio between the inhalations and the exhalations. With practice, you can prolong the exhalations further, to ratios of 1:1.5 and then 1:2.

Bhramari Pranayama (Honey Bee Humming)

• Keep hands in the Chin Mudra touching the tip of index finger with the tip of the thumb, or comfortably place one palm on top of the other in the lap.

• Adopt the Khechari Mudra by touching the tip of the tongue to the roof of the closed mouth.

• Inhale and chant 'MM' or 'NN' and feel the vibrations in the head and the face.

• Repeat with an inhalation.

• Never over-chant. Feeling the relaxing vibrations is more important than the duration of the chant.

Mental Programming

• Affirmation

• Visualization

Attitude of Gratitude

References

Psychophysiological States: The Ultradian Dynamics of Mind-Body Interactions – Dr. David S. Shannahoff-Khalsa, International Review of Neurobiology, Volume 80

From Medication to Meditation - Osho

Scientific Healing Affirmations - Paramhansa Yogananda

The Healing Path of Yoga – Nischala Joy Devi

Quantum Healing: Exploring the Frontiers of Mind/Body Medicine - Deepak Chopra

Prana, Pranayama, Prana Vidya – Swami Niranjananda Saraswati, Bihar School of Yoga

Pranayama: The Art and Science – Dr. H. R. Nagendra, Vivekananda Kendra Yoga Prakashan, Bangalore

Breath, Mind and Consciousness - Harish Johari

Destructive Emotions and How We Can Overcome Them – Dalai Lama and Daniel Goleman

Getting Well Again – O. Carl Simonton

Practicing the Power of Now – Eckhart Tolle

The Power of Your Subconscious Mind – Dr. Joseph Murphy

The Silva Mind Control Method – Jose Silva

Mind Power – Christian H. Godefroy

JAICO PUBLISHING HOUSE

Elevate Your Life. Transform Your World.

Established in 1946, Jaico Publishing House is the publisher of stellar authors such as Sri Sri Paramahansa Yogananda, Osho, Robin Sharma, Deepak Chopra, Stephen Hawking, Eknath Easwaran, Sarvapalli Radhakrishnan, Nirad Chaudhuri, Khushwant Singh, Mulk Raj Anand, John Maxwell, Ken Blanchard and Brian Tracy. Our list which has crossed a landmark 2000 titles, is amongst the most diverse in the country, with books in religion, spirituality, mind/body/spirit, self-help, business, cookery, humour, career, games, biographies, fiction, and science.

Jaico has expanded its horizons to become a leading publisher of educational and professional books in management and engineering. Our college-level textbooks and reference titles are used by students countrywide. The success of our academic and professional titles is largely due to the efforts of our Educational and Corporate Sales Divisions.

The late Mr. Jaman Shah established Jaico as a book distribution company. Sensing that independence was around the corner, he aptly named his company Jaico ("Jai" means victory in Hindi). In order to tap the significant demand for affordable books in a developing nation, Mr. Shah initiated Jaico's own publications. Jaico was India's first publisher of paperback books in the English language.

In addition to being a publisher and distributor of its own titles, Jaico is a major distributor of books of leading international publishers such as McGraw Hill, Pearson, Cengage Learning, John Wiley and Elsevier Science. With its headquarters in Mumbai, Jaico has other sales offices in Ahmedabad, Bangalore, Bhopal, Chennai, Delhi, Hyderabad and Kolkata. Our sales team of over 40 executives, direct mail order division, and website ensure that our books effectively reach all urban and rural parts of the country.

SINCE 1946